The Failure of Global Capitalism
From Cape Breton to Colombia and Beyond

Cape Breton University Press recognizes the support of the Canada Council for the Arts, Block Grant program, and the Province of Nova Scotia, through the Department of Tourism, Culture and Heritage, for our publishing program. We are pleased to work in partnership with these bodies to develop and promote our cultural resources.

Canada Council   Conseil des Arts
for the Arts   du Canada

NOVA SCOTIA
Tourism, Culture and Heritage

Cover: Cathy MacLean Design, Newtown, NS
         Artwork by Catherine Hughes (see note page 6)
First printed in Canada

Library and Archives Canada Cataloguing in Publication
Gibbs, Terry, 1967-
    The failure of global capitalism : from Cape Breton to Colombia and beyond / Terry Gibbs and Garry Leech.
Includes bibliographical references and index.

ISBN 978-1-897009-32-1 :c$19.95
    1. Globalization--Economic aspects--Case studies. 2. Capitalism.
3. Neoliberalism. 4. International business enterprises--Developing countries. 5. Coal mines and mining--Nova Scotia--Cape Breton Island. 6. Coal mines and mining--Colombia. 7. International economic relations.
I. Leech, Garry, 1960- II. Title.
HC59.3.G52 2009   330.9   C2009-900331-7

Cape Breton University Press
P.O. Box 5300
Sydney, Nova Scotia B1P 6L2
Canada

The Failure of Global Capitalism
From Cape Breton to Colombia and Beyond

Terry Gibbs and Garry Leech

Cape Breton University Press
Sydney, Nova Scotia, Canada

This book is dedicated to our sons, Owen and Morgan, and to the future.

About the cover

Artwork by Catherine Hughes, inspired by the Atlantic Regional Solidarity Network's Mining the Connections Campaign to oppose gold and coal mining operations in Guatemala and Colombia, which are harming individual lives, communities and the environment for the sake, directly or indirectly, of profits in Canada.

Achi sentence: "M'i Yaij be' la kl'eoj" by Jeremias Tecu. Translation: "Don't steal what belongs to us." Achi is an indigenous Mayan language spoken in Guatemala.

Mi'kmaq sentence: "Puni Emeko'tmnej Kmitkinu" by Phyllis Googoo. Translation: "Do not destroy our world" or "Respect our world."

"!Basta ya!" is Spanish, meaning "Enough already!"

Contents

Acknowledgements

We would first like to acknowledge our students, colleagues and friends in Cape Breton who have contributed significantly to our understanding of this beautiful island and have influenced our worldview. We would like to thank Sean Howard, Steve Law, Don MacGillivray, Suzanne MacNeil, James Sacouman, Scott Sinclair and Tom Urbaniak for their insightful readings of the manuscript and valuable suggestions. We give our special thanks to Aviva Chomsky for contributing the foreword to the book and are eternally grateful to Catherine Hughes for allowing us to use her inspiring artwork on the cover. We would also like to thank Mike Hunter of Cape Breton University Press for his thoughtful comments on the manuscript and for his faith in the book. Finally, we would like to acknowledge the following friends and colleagues whose insights into Atlantic Canada and/or Colombia over the years proved invaluable to us in the writing of this book: Kathryn Anderson, Wilf Bean, James J. Brittain, Lee-Anne Broadhead, Evan Coole, Remedios Fajardo, James Guy, Brian Howe, Adam Isacson, David Johnson, Evelyn Jones, Victoria Maldonado, Andrew Molloy, Barb Moore, Mario A. Murillo, Liliany Obando, Armando Pérez, Jose Julio Pérez, Lisandro Pérez, Francisco Ramírez, Ardelle Reynolds, Steve Striffler and Mike Targett.

There are numerous other Colombian friends who we would also like to thank; sadly, they cannot be named for security reasons.

"From Moses and Jesus and Marx and Carlyle, one outstanding theme runs thru all their teachings, however much the language employed may have differed. The sins which all of them denounced most fiercely were economic sins, and the mission of all of them in life was to deliver the oppressed."

James Bryson McLachlan, 1919

Foreword

Aviva Chomsky

Why is it that the rich seem to be getting richer, and the poor poorer? Why are working conditions and social services deteriorating around the world? Who really benefits when production moves from the global North to the global South? Who makes the economic decisions affecting all of our lives? And what can we do about it? If you've ever wondered about any of these questions, you've picked up the right book.

It has become a truism to speak of our world as interlinked, globalized. But rarely has a study done such an excellent job of untangling the myriad skeins actually constituting these linkages and of revealing how people in two different regions are caught up in a single, global economic process.

Using the case studies of Atlantic Canada and Colombia, Terry Gibbs and Garry Leech trace the evolution of our industrial system and explain how the current neoliberal era affects people in both the North and the South. In Cape Breton, the coal and steel industries that once created an industrial economy and a working class have closed; in Colombia, neoliberal economic policies have invited in multinational mining companies that export coal back to the North, including to Nova Scotia itself. We see the two sides of the neoliberal coin: workers in Cape Breton struggle with the loss of jobs and services, while workers and communities in Colombia struggle with the depredations of unrestricted global capitalism. The rights and benefits that workers in both the North and the South struggled for over the course of the 20th century are lost, as companies seek ever higher profits.

One key theme in the book is the effect of industrial development on the environment. Both capitalism and state socialism have promoted development models based on the idea that more is better, that living standards must constantly rise. But the planet's resources are finite, and the coal that links Cape Breton with Colombia offers a perfect example of the fallacy of a development model that is based on extracting and destroying a resource, devastating the local environment and the earth's atmosphere—and leaving nothing positive to show for it when the company is gone.

But Gibbs and Leech are not content just to provide a coherent—and bleak—analysis of global capitalism. They also look at a variety of alternatives, ranging from state socialism to local collectives—including those in both Nova Scotia and Colombia—that have sought to place human needs above profits. By showing us with such crystal clarity what is wrong with our world, they also make a convincing case that another world is possible.

The authors have lived and travelled extensively in the regions they describe and have witnessed, participated in and spoken with the actors involved in many of the events they have included here. Their book offers a unique combination of engaging first-hand reporting and cogent historical and political analysis. This is a book, and an experience, worth savouring. You will learn; you will be outraged; you will be uplifted.

Aviva Chomsky is a history professor and the coordinator of Latin American studies at Salem State College, Salem, MA.

Introduction

The Impossible Dream

On picking up this book, a potential reader's first response might be: What on earth do Cape Breton and Colombia have in common? At first glance, it appears not much. At least that was our initial impression when we moved to Cape Breton in August 2004. After all, Cape Breton is a relatively small island located off the northeastern tip of mainland Nova Scotia in Canada. It is home to 145,000 people—mostly indigenous Mi'kmaq, Acadians and descendents of Scottish and Irish immigrants. In contrast, Colombia is a geographically diverse nation in tropical South America, with a population of forty-four million, the majority of whom are Mestizos—a Spanish and indigenous mix—with most of the remainder being Afro-Colombians and indigenous. The two places appear to be at opposite ends of the Americas, both literally and figuratively.

Before moving to Cape Breton, most of our research had been conducted in Latin America, studying the consequences of neoliberal—or so-called free market—globalization for people and communities in that region of the global South.[1] Shortly after our arrival in Cape Breton, we began to notice many social and economic similarities between our new home and Colombia. The most obvious connection between the two regions is coal. Coal mining had been the backbone of Cape Breton's economy for more than one hundred years. However, the last mine was shut down in 2001 when the province's utility company, Nova Scotia Power (NSP), took advantage of neoliberal globalization by importing coal from Colombia. It seemed to us to be a perfect example of the loss of well-paid, unionized industrial jobs in the global North—primarily North America and Europe—due to globalization having established the conditions that allow multinational corporations to more profitably exploit the natural resources of the global South—Latin America, Africa and Asia. But the commonalities between Cape Breton and Colombia do not end with coal; there are numerous others also directly related to the capitalist system: militant labour struggles, repression, economic insecurity, population displacement, remittances, social inequality and environmental devastation.

Under globalization, capitalist elites—primarily multinational corporations, investment banks and international financial institutions, along with the politicians and conservative think tanks that serve their interests—have pushed a one-size-fits-all economic model on nations in both the North and the South. The objective has been to establish a global free-market economic system. As a result, nations of the North have become intrinsically linked to countries in the South because globalization has eradicated borders to facilitate the exploitation of natural resources, labour and the production and consumption of goods. For many working in the financial centres of the global capitalist system—New York, Los Angeles, London, Paris, Tokyo, Toronto and to a lesser degree other large cities including Colombia's capital, Bogotá—neoliberalism has been a bonanza as corporations have achieved record profits, and stock markets have soared. For many living on the periphery of the global economy, however, places such as Cape Breton and rural Colombia that have traditionally relied on the exploitation of their natural resources, globalization has proven to be socially and economically devastating.

Whereas Cape Breton and Colombia obviously possess unique cultural and geographic traits, significantly influencing the economic and social realities of each place, they both function in the same global capitalist economy. In many ways, they epitomize the reality faced by countries in both the global North and the global South struggling to cope with the neoliberal model. Cape Breton's industrialization experience during the liberal era of capitalism and its deindustrialization under neoliberalism parallels that of many other post-industrial communities in the global North. Similarly, the advent of neoliberalism and the consequent opening up of Colombia's economy—and by extension its workers and natural resources—to exploitation by multinational corporations reflect many aspects of the reality experienced by nations throughout the global South. While the central theme of the book is the failure of global capitalism, Cape Breton and Colombia constitute the North-South thread running through the narrative. These two regions are necessarily situated to varying degrees within their geopolitical contexts. It is impossible, for instance, to look at Cape Breton without examining its provincial and national contexts. Similarly, neoliberalism in Colombia cannot be addressed in isolation, either from the emergence of that particular economic model throughout the global South, or from the alternatives appearing in countries such as Venezuela.

We are told that the neoliberal economic model that dominates the globalization process is inevitable and evolutionary, and that it will ultimately elevate the standards of living of everyone in the world. But is neoliberalism really inevitable? Is it a natural evolution of human civilization? And will it ultimately improve the material conditions of everyone? We argue in this book that neoliberalism is not inevitable, but rather that it is a conscious, ideologically motivated set of policies. In fact, the only "inevitable" aspects of this economic model are that it is environmentally unsustainable and it increases the wealth of the world's capitalist elites at the expense of the majority in both the North and the South. We argue that the profit imperative inherent in not only the neoliberal model, but in capitalism itself, renders the system unsustainable from both a socio-economic and an environmental perspective. Consequently, the dream being pitched by capitalist elites to people in the South—that through neoliberalism they can attain the same standards of living as that enjoyed in the North—amounts to nothing more than that: a dream. The impossible dream.

Because of the global nature of neoliberalism, local efforts in Cape Breton, Colombia and throughout the world to turn the impossible dream into a sustainable reality often fail. We argue that far-reaching structural changes are required at the local, national and international levels if we are to achieve a sustainable and more egalitarian alternative to global capitalism. After all, under neoliberalism, as sociologist William I. Robinson has noted:

> There is a new configuration of global power that becomes manifest in each nation and whose tentacles reach all the way down to the community level. Each individual, each nation, and each region is being drawn into transnational processes that have un-

dermined the earlier autonomies and provincialisms. This makes it entirely impossible to address local issues removed from global context.[2]

Ultimately, this book is about the linkages between the local and the global. To be more precise, it is about understanding these connections and the necessity of acting both locally and globally if we are to move beyond the global capitalist model.

The first three chapters examine the socio-economic inequalities and injustices inherent in the global capitalist system, while chapter four looks at the environmental unsustainability of capitalism and at potential alternatives. Chapter one begins by placing neoliberalism in Canada in its historical context. It introduces the anti-capitalist struggles of Cape Breton's militant miners and steelworkers during the liberal era and then looks at the establishment of the Fordist compact under the broader Keynesian policy framework. That chapter concludes by illustrating how the profit imperative inherent in capitalism inevitably led to the dismantling of the Fordist compact and the undermining of the so-called welfare state in the 1980s under the banner of neoliberalism. In Cape Breton, neoliberal globalization led to the closing of the local steel plant and coal mines—the latter resulting, in part, from Nova Scotia Power (NSP) importing cheaper coal from Colombia.

Chapter two looks at how, following the end of the Cold War, the U.S. government and Washington-based international financial institutions such as the International Monetary Fund (IMF) and the World Bank sought to dismantle Colombia's Keynesian-inspired import substitution industrialization (ISI) model, which had been in place since the middle decades of the 20th century. In the post-Cold War era, pro-neoliberal governments in Colombia have implemented economic reforms that have proven devastating for much of the population. These economic policies have made Colombia's natural resources, particularly oil and coal, available for exploitation by multinational corporations. As a result, rural communities have experienced increased levels of violence and human rights abuses as they have been driven from their resource-rich lands. One such community was the Afro-Colombian town of Tabaco, whose residents were forcibly displaced to allow for the expansion of the Cerrejón mine, which provides coal to NSP and other customers in North America and Europe.

Meanwhile, with NSP no longer purchasing local coal, the economy of Cape Breton shifted from being industrial-based to being "knowledge" based. Chapter three examines how U.S. corporations have taken advantage of favourable investment conditions under globalization by establishing their customer service operations in call centres located throughout Atlantic Canada. These multinational companies have exploited the surplus of cheap labour in post-industrial communities such as Cape Breton. As a result, social inequalities have grown not only in Cape Breton, but throughout Canada, as many corporations are earning record profits while increasing numbers of workers are forced out of well-paid, unionized manufacturing jobs and into low-paid, non-unionized service sector work. These same neoliberal reforms have cut funding for healthcare, education and other social programs, thereby imposing further hardships on a majority of the population.

In chapter four, we look at potential alternatives to global capitalism. We examine alternatives that are currently challenging neoliberal capitalist structures and that could provide inspiration and ideas to people in Cape Breton, Colombia and throughout the world. We look at the State-led challenge to neoliberalism currently under way in Venezuela, particularly government policies that seek to redistribute the national wealth to benefit the poor majority. We also analyze the model of participatory democracy that has emerged in Venezuela and the empowerment of people that can occur when a national government prioritizes the needs of the poor over those of capitalist elites. The chapter also looks at how global capitalism's dependence on fossil fuels has made the model environmentally unsustainable and concludes by examining the mostly self-sufficient, sustainable and egalitarian community of Las Gaviotas in rural Colombia. Finally, we look at the role that most of us play in preserving the current economic structures. More specifically, we examine the need to re-evaluate our consumer lifestyles—particularly in the North—and we look at the importance of engaging in collective action to successfully challenge the structures of global capitalism.

The information in this book is drawn from a variety of sources, including interviews, government and non-governmental reports, media accounts and other publications. The perspectives presented are also influenced by our own experiences and observations from the past four years spent living in Cape Breton and from many years of work in Latin America, particularly Colombia.

We believe the examples of Cape Breton and Colombia illustrate many of the harsh realities experienced by people in both the North and the South under global capitalism. It is our hope that this book will help people better understand not only the connections between the global North and the global South, but also the common experiences of many peoples throughout the world under capitalism, particularly with regard to socio-economic and environmental issues. Ultimately, it is our hope that the story herein will contribute in some small way to the establishment of a new global economic model, one that is infinitely more sustainable and egalitarian than global capitalism.

One

The Rise and Fall of Industrial Capitalism in Cape Breton

On January 1, 1994, the North American Free Trade Agreement (NAFTA) went into effect. While it was the best-known expression of neoliberalism in Canada at that time—and remains so today—it was neither the first nor the only one. Shortly after becoming prime minister in 1984, Conservative Party leader Brian Mulroney visited the United States and announced to more than one thousand corporate executives attending a dinner in New York City that "Canada is open for business again."[1] Mulroney quickly ensured that Canada was moving rapidly along the same neoliberal trajectory as the United States and Britain, governed by his ideological allies President Ronald Reagan and Prime Minister Margaret Thatcher respectively. By 1989, the Mulroney government had signed the Canada-United States free trade agreement, privatized twenty-three of Canada's sixty-one Crown corporations and shifted more of the tax burden away from corporations and to individuals by introducing the goods and services tax (GST). Essentially, the neoliberal ideology had already become entrenched in Ottawa by the time Mulroney signed NAFTA in December 1992. In the ensuing years, both the Conservative and Liberal parties would become strong advocates of neoliberalism. The hegemony of the free-market discourse also became entrenched in the Republican and Democratic parties in the United States and the Conservative and Labour parties in Britain, as the dominant political parties in all three nations quickly fell into step.

The implementation of neoliberalism in Canada in many ways harkens a return to the classical liberal era of capitalism, which was epitomized by gross inequalities in wealth as a small minority amassed huge fortunes at the expense of the mass of humanity enduring Dickensian misery. At the beginning of the 20th century, nowhere in Canada was the contrast and conflict between wealthy industrial barons and the impoverished working class more apparent than in Cape Breton. In the early decades of the century, two of Canada's more militant unions—the coalminers and steelworkers in Cape Breton—sought to change the capitalist structures they saw as responsible for the gross social and economic inequalities so prevalent at the time.

The Cape Breton Radicals

During the early part of the 20th century, Canada's economic trajectory differed from those of the U.S. and U.K., in that its industrial sector was not the country's economic mainstay. In Canada, the exploitation of the country's vast natural resources constituted the most prominent component of its economic activity, leading Canadian economist Harold Innis to develop the staples theory. Innis noted that the staples of the Canadian economy were its natural resources, which were mostly exploited for export, thereby keeping the nation on the periphery of the international economy rather than at its industrial centre.[2] The staples theory was particularly applicable to Atlantic Canada, where the fishing, mining and lumber sectors drove the region's economy. However, despite the region's economic reliance on natural resource extraction, a manufacturing sector did develop, although often to support the extractive industries. For instance, steel plants were constructed in coal-mining regions such as Cape Breton and fish-processing plants were established in coastal areas throughout Atlantic Canada.

The industrialization process in Nova Scotia mostly represented a response to the growing national demand for coal, iron and steel. Much of the steel being consumed in Canada at the beginning of the 20th century was imported from the United States and Britain. To be perceived as a modern industrial nation it was considered crucial for Canada to have a domestic steel industry. After all, copious amounts of steel were required to manufacture the products symbolic of a modern nation: railway engines, railway lines, ships, automobiles and bridges, among other things.

The alliance between government, on both the provincial and federal levels, and corporations quickly became apparent, as public funds were generously handed over to the private sector to help facilitate the industrialization process. In 1892, Boston financier Henry Melville Whitney obtained from Nova Scotia's Liberal government the exclusive rights to most of the coal on Cape Breton Island for ninety-nine years and established the Dominion Coal Company. A decade later, Whitney founded the Dominion Iron and Steel Company (DISCO) and set about building a steel plant in Sydney, Cape Breton. Whitney received not only grants from every level of government, he was also given five hundred acres of prime waterfront property, sixty-five million gallons a day of free water for the plant's operations and a thirty-year exemption from municipal taxes.[3]

The building of the massive steel plant dramatically transformed Sydney, from a small, quiet port town with a population of 2,427 in 1891 to an industrial city of 18,000 by 1911.[4] Sydney and the surrounding coal communities became quintessential company towns and the well-being of the local citizenry was intimately linked to the ups and downs of the steel and coal industries, which were themselves closely interconnected. Both the Dominion Coal Company and DISCO established company housing, and the coal-mining towns also contained company stores. While some have called such practices "welfare capitalism," they were in fact far from altruistic. Indeed, they helped ensure the complete dependence of workers on the company because unsatisfactory job performance, participation in work slowdowns or strikes, or organizing a union could mean not only loss of employment, but also homelessness for labourers and their families.

Working and living conditions for steelworkers and miners during the first three decades of the 20th century closely resembled the Dickensian misery of Victorian-era Britain. A 1913 housing study of Whitney Pier, a largely immigrant neighbourhood in Sydney, discovered appalling population densities in many dwellings. According to the study, 331 Poles and Russians were living in 19 houses, while 257 Italians resided in another 19 houses nearby. The study also revealed that many Newfoundlanders who had come to Sydney to work at the steel plant lived in wooden shacks, despite the harsh winter climate. According to the report:

Some of the houses are fairly clean, but the majority are exceedingly filthy. There is no sewerage or water connections, and the ventilation is foul. Especially is this true in some shacks at the coloured quarters, which are occupied, not by Negroes, but by Hungarians, Poles and Newfoundlanders.[5]

Many of the steel plant's workers had to endure such horrendous living conditions because of the low wages they earned. In the early part of the century, steelworkers were paid an average of 15 cents an hour—2.5 cents an hour less than the amount that the Sydney city council decreed to be a fair minimum wage in 1910.[6] Work in the steel plant was hard, the hours long. Workers had to endure shifts of eleven and thirteen hours a day, seven days a week. According to historian Craig Heron, this allowed the owners to hire fewer workers than if they had eight-hour shifts, and it ensured that the company controlled the entire lives of the labourers, because they only had time to work and sleep.[7] One former steel worker who routinely worked seventy-two hours a week declared, "It was a hell of a way to spend your youth, just on the job all the time."[8]

Like Canada's other manufacturing corporations, DISCO was an ardent opponent of legislative attempts to introduce the eight-hour workday because it would increase labour costs. In 1910, one steel plant superintendent defended the long workdays by telling a parliamentary committee, "We get better results from our men where we have them work 11 and 13 hours." He then claimed that reducing the lengths of the shifts and not having employees work on Sundays and holidays "seems to give them too much time off; too much chance of spending money and to get around."[9]

The company also worked hard to discourage its workers from organizing. It established a network of spies in the plant to report information to the company's private police force, which in turn worked hand-in-hand with local law enforcement. In the early years, workers who tried to organize risked losing their jobs. Even after a union was finally established, the leaders of unsuccessful strikes still faced the possibility of being fired and blacklisted, which ensured that they would not find work at any other steel plant. As Heron points out:

All of this repressive apparatus in Canada's steel plants was intended to prevent the development of any collective power among the workers that could effectively challenge managerial authority. The entire administration of the corporations' labour policies was premised on the steelworkers' complete subservience to their bosses.... Fundamentally, these practices rested on manipulation of the fear of unemployment and poverty that a large pool of surplus labour outside the plant gates made possible at most times.[10]

Sydney's steelworkers finally succeeded in their efforts to organize, and became part of the Amalgamated Association of Iron, Steel and Tin Workers in 1917. One of the reasons that the Sydney plant and other Canadian factories had been so successful in preventing workers from organizing up to that point was the alliance between the economic elites and the government in Ottawa. Canada's federal government proved to be even more anti-union than its neighbour south of the border, as evidenced by the rulings of royal commissions, which repeatedly sided with employers in labour disputes.[11] It was only the huge demand for steel during the First World War that finally provided the workers with the necessary leverage to successfully organize. But while the workers had established a union, the Sydney plant's owners still refused to recognize it or to engage in collective bargaining.

One of the concerns of the steel plant's owners was the fact that the newly organized workers not only wanted the eight-hour workday and the right to bargain collectively, but that they also sought to establish an "industrial democracy." The economic model envisioned by the workers included their involvement in management and in the decision-making processes of the workplace. In other words, Nova Scotia's steelworkers, unlike most of their colleagues in Ontario, actually dared to challenge the capitalist model. As Heron notes, "Only in Nova Scotia did the leaders of the steelworkers' unions question the legitimacy of corporate ownership and control."[12] Cape Breton's steelworkers were inspired in part by the island's militant coal miners.

In 1917, a socialist miner named James Bryson McLachlan, who had arrived in Cape Breton from Scotland in 1902, finally succeeded in convincing many of the region's miners to abandon the Provincial Workmens' Association (PWA), which most mineworkers saw as a company union. For almost a decade, McLachlan and like-minded miners had fought against both the company, by engaging in strikes among other things, and the PWA, by trying to establish a new union. Finally, the miners joined the newly created

District 26 of the U.S.-based United Mine Workers of America (UMWA), which had won the eight-hour workday for coal workers in the United States in 1898—Cape Breton miners still worked twelve-hour shifts. McLachlan and the other leaders of District 26 were far more radical than their counterparts in the PWA. Although, as historian Don MacGillivray points out, it was not only the new union's leaders who were radical, but a significant portion of the rank and file too—in fact, many proved to be even more militant than their leaders.[13]

The Dominion Coal Company, under pressure from the government, which was concerned with potential production interruptions impeding the country's war effort, reluctantly recognized the new union. As expected, the union's first act was to reiterate the miners' long-standing demand for the eight-hour workday. The battle for a shorter working day was being fought in many industries throughout Canada. In fact, almost half of the 219 strikes nationwide in 1919 were for shorter hours, including the Winnipeg General Strike.[14] Recognizing the unity of the members of District 26, evident in the 98 per cent vote by members in favour of joining the UMWA, the Dominion Coal Company relented and agreed to the eight-hour workday for Cape Breton's coal miners in 1919.[15]

McLachlan and his allies, however, were not content to limit their battles to the workplace; their broader objective was to challenge the capitalist system. In late 1917, McLachlan helped establish the Independent Labour Party of Nova Scotia and became its first president. The party's anti-capitalist stance was evident in its mission statement: "To give expression politically to the hopes and aspirations of the working class alone and by use of the ballot to establish working class ownership and democratic management of all social means of wealth production and distribution at the earliest possible date."[16]

In municipal elections in the Cape Breton mining town of New Waterford, held on February 5, 1918, the Independent Labour Party received an overwhelming mandate and became the first workers' party to gain control of a government in the Maritimes. The victory drew strong reactions from local elites in nearby Sydney. Following the election, the headline of the *Sydney Record* demanded, "Government Should Take Immediate Action to Clear Out Nest of Red

Vipers!"[17] The article called for military intervention to overthrow the newly elected New Waterford government.

In 1920, the Independent Labour Party allied itself with the United Farmers of Nova Scotia Party for the upcoming provincial elections. While McLachlan declined to be a candidate, he was nonetheless engaged in the political debates during the campaign. At a gathering of striking Halifax dockworkers, the union leader reiterated the importance of workers organizing beyond the workplace to achieve revolutionary change in Canada:

> What is needed is political action by the workers to the end that their own representatives, members of the working class, are elected to parliament and all public bodies. This will be the next big move of the working class, and every worker must become conscious of his own power and educate and acquaint himself with social and economic questions, so that when the time arrives for Labour to take over the administration of public affairs the great bulk of the people will be ready to advance into the great cooperative commonwealth.[18]

The combined labour-farmer ticket received significant support from disenchanted workers and farmers, sweeping the four seats in Cape Breton County and winning a total of eleven seats throughout Nova Scotia. Still, it did not gain a majority and the new Liberal government was mostly successful in blocking the new party's motions in the provincial legislature.

The success of the labour-farmer ticket at the provincial ballot box nevertheless led the parties to nominate candidates for the upcoming federal elections. The British Empire Steel Corporation (BESCO)—which had become the owner of the Sydney steel plant and the local coal mines in 1920—was concerned with the socialist leanings of the labour-farmer ticket. The company launched a campaign of intimidation against the ticket's candidates, some of whom, like McLachlan, were leaders of District 26. During the campaign BESCO increased its spying activities, as well as firings and blacklistings. Company president Roy Wolvin even threatened to shut down both the steel plant and the coal mines because of "the alarming growth of Communism."[19] And then, on December 1, 1921, with the election only two weeks away, Wolvin partly followed through on his threat and abruptly closed seven mines. BESCO's ally, the provincial Liberal Party, criticized the federal Conservative government for allowing such an economic catastrophe to occur and told Nova Scotians that the only way to get the mines open again would be to elect a Liberal government to Ottawa. The party also dispatched food wagons to Cape Breton to provide "aid" to the suffering miners and their families.

At the same time, the Liberals implemented a smear campaign against McLachlan, claiming that the union leader had secretly sold out his members in negotiations with the company that were ongoing at the time. On the morning of the election, the headline of the *Sydney Post* declared that McLachlan's Liberal Party opponent, Billy Carroll, had produced "conclusive proof" of these charges at a debate between the two candidates held the previous evening. In actuality, Carroll had done no such thing, and it quickly became apparent that no such proof existed. The *Sydney Post* ignored this inconvenient fact, however, and published the damning headline anyway. The paper's owners decided not to sell the paper on the day of the election, but to give it away. When the ballots were counted, Carroll had defeated McLachlan by a narrow margin.[20] Local political and economic elites—represented by the Liberal Party, BESCO and the *Sydney Post*—had successfully used their wealth and power to preserve their positions of privilege.

Meanwhile, Sydney's steelworkers continued to demand the right to collective bargaining, the eight-hour workday and higher wages, engaging in several strikes in the early 1920s with little success. According to one worker at the Sydney plant, "You could spend your life there, but they weren't obligated at any time to give you more pay. [...] If you wanted a raise you waited until somebody died or quit, but few people quit. They lasted as long as they could. I worked with one fellow that was nearly 90, old Bob MacLellan. He just couldn't afford to quit."[21]

In February 1923, the steelworkers again walked out when the company refused to reinstate an employee whom the union claimed had been wrongfully dismissed. The company's president Wolvin blamed what he called "Cape Breton Bolshevism" for the strike and issued an ultimatum to local political and business leaders, threatening to permanently shut down the steel plant if the radicals weren't driven out of Cape Breton. Ultimately, despite the issuance of a proclamation by the local Board of Trade against the so-called Cape

Breton Bolshevists, the radicals prevailed and the company agreed to review the firing and offered the steelworkers a 10-per-cent raise, which was only half the amount of a pay cut they suffered the previous year.[22]

Once production in the plant returned to normal, the company declared that the firing was valid and dispatched the employee in question to the United States. It also announced its commitment to a non-unionized workplace and got warrants issued for the arrest of thirty-five steelworkers accused of blocking trains from entering the plant during the strike. The provincial government declared Cape Breton County a police district and authorized the deployment of up to one thousand officers to Sydney. The police officers were billeted inside the plant and repeatedly made forays into town to raid the homes of union leaders. Meanwhile, politicians and the media launched a campaign to portray the union leaders as irresponsible citizens and revolutionaries. According to Heron, "Not since the Winnipeg General Strike had Canada seen such a well-coordinated campaign by the state, media, and private industry to destroy a workers' organization."[23]

Undeterred, the union again approached the company with demands that included a 20 per cent pay increase and recognition of the union. BESCO refused to consider the new demands and, on June 28, 1923, the steelworkers walked out. Confrontations ensued outside the plant's gate between huge crowds of picketers and local police. In response, the premier redeployed the provincial police to Sydney along with fifteen hundred soldiers, who were stationed at the plant. According to Heron:

> The crowds of picketing strikers now faced a formidable force of military might and soon found themselves staring down the barrels of machine guns and scurrying out of the way of men on horseback wielding clubs and sabres. On Sunday, July 1, the provincial police made a particularly violent assault on an unorganized crowd of unarmed strikers and churchgoers returning from evening service on the main street of Whitney Pier.[24]

In response to "Bloody Sunday," Cape Breton's coal miners walked off the job to protest the use of military force against the steelworkers and their families. In a letter announcing the sympathy strike to local unions, McLachlan declared:

On Sunday night last these Provincial Police in the most brutal manner rode down the people at Whitney Pier who were on the street, most of whom were coming from Church. Neither age, sex or physical disabilities were proof against these brutes. One old woman over seventy years of age was beaten into insensibility and may die. A boy nine years old was trampled under the horses' feet and his breastbone crushed in. One woman was beaten of the head with a police club and gave premature birth to a child. The child is dead and the woman's life is despaired of. Men and women were beaten up inside their own homes. Against the brutes the miners are on strike. The Government of Nova Scotia is the guilty and responsible party for this crime.[25]

Even though miners in Alberta walked out in solidarity with the Cape Breton mineworkers' sympathy strike, Nova Scotia's provincial government remained undeterred. In fact, the government intensified the repression by arresting McLachlan on charges of seditious libel for statements contained in the letter to the local unions. Upon his arrest, the union leader was whisked out of Cape Breton to stand trial in Halifax, which was not only far away from his home base but was also not the constituency where he allegedly committed the crime. McLachlan was eventually convicted and sentenced to six years in prison.

The international president of the United Mine Workers of America, John L. Lewis, a moderate who was looking for an excuse to remove the radical union leaders in Cape Breton, took advantage of the fact that McLachlan was sitting in a Halifax jail cell, and declared the miners' sympathy strike to be in violation of their collective agreement. Taking advantage of Lewis's intervention with the miners, BESCO took a hard line with the steelworkers by breaking off negotiations. A month into the strike, the company announced that strikers would be evicted from company housing. Almost two years of pay cuts and layoffs had depleted the financial reserves of the steelworkers and so, with the strikers and their families facing hunger and eviction from their homes, the union decided to end the strike. The company immediately fired and blacklisted the union's leaders, forcing many of them to leave Cape Breton to search for work. Workers who participated in the strike were given the worst jobs in the plant when they returned to work. The government blamed the strike and its related violence on "communist infiltrators."

The 1923 strike broke the back of the steelworkers' union in Sydney. As Heron notes:

> The steelworkers' post-war vision of 'industrial democracy' had finally been smashed. The steelmaking corporations had vigorously rejected the idea that their workers might exercise some formal power in co-determining workplace policies. With the active assistance and collaboration of the Canadian State, the corporations had re-established their systems of hierarchical, authoritarian control, which left the workers in a state of fearful dependence and vulnerability.[26]

It would be more than a decade before the steelworkers would finally obtain the eight-hour workday.

The "state of fearful dependence and vulnerability," described by Heron, was made evident in a 1929 *Sydney Post* article noting that steady work would be available for only 2,800 of the plant's 3,600 employees. This inevitably resulted in a large pool of surplus labour, which contributed to reducing wages and undermining job security for those who were working. As one retired steelworker later recalled, "You couldn't spend money you earned because if you were going to get laid off, there was no unemployment insurance."[27]

Workers could not expect financial or political support from the State. Both the provincial and federal governments had repeatedly made clear their sympathy for the owners of the steel and coal industries through their military deployments, court rulings, commissions and declarations. During a 1925 coal miners' strike, BESCO cut off credit at company stores and shut down the water and electricity supply to the mining town of New Waterford. Following the killing of a striking miner, Bill Davis, by a company police officer, frustrated and angry workers looted and burned down several company stores. At one point, a BESCO vice-president was asked if the company would reduce the selling price of coal to consumers if the miners accepted a reduction in wages. He unabashedly replied, "No. We require the money for our bondholders and shareholders."[28]

The government established the Royal Commission on the Coal Mining Industry in Nova Scotia to investigate the strike. The Commission's final report clearly reflected Ottawa's allegiance to the company, recommending a 10-per-cent pay cut for the miners and declaring:

The operators run the mines to make profit, the miners dig coal to make a living, and these two ends just won't jibe under present conditions. The miners want a living, the operators want profits. Which of these two "wants" should receive the prime and first consideration? The commission, this unprejudiced commission, has left no doubt on that question. Profits come first, and these must be maintained even if the present low standard of living of the coal miners has to be reduced still further.[29]

By the time the commission released its report, both Cape Breton's steelworkers and its coal miners had, for the most part, failed in their goal to radically change the capitalist structures and to bring into existence an industrial democracy to ensure that workers had at least some control over the means of production. With the removal of McLachlan and other radical local union leaders, the more moderate, anti-militant approach of the UMWA's international department prevailed among the new labour leaders in Cape Breton. Class collaborators in Canada's union movement heralded the downfall of Cape Breton's militant labour leaders. Following the 1925 coal miners' strike, Tom Moore, president of the Trades and Labour Congress of Canada (TLC), declared, "The days of red leadership among Nova Scotia miners are ended."[30]

From Confrontation to Collaboration

While militant unionists in Cape Breton and throughout Canada would continue the struggle to restructure capitalism in the ensuing decades, they would never achieve the leadership positions that radicals like McLachlan had held earlier. For the most part, unions avoided overly militant actions, with the exception of a brief resurgence of radicalism in the 1930s. They focused primarily on wages and working conditions and placed far less emphasis on achieving radical political and economic changes at the national and international levels. Class collaboration became the order of the day, as owners and workers engaged in what became known as the Fordist compact.

In this environment, capitalist owners recognized unions and granted wage and benefit concessions to workers. The benefits to the owners were fewer production interruptions, resulting from labour unrest, and more consumers for their goods, due to the higher incomes earned by their workers. On the other side of the compact, says political scientist Thom Workman, "Labour achieved real gains for working people throughout the North but stopped well short of challenging the general system of class exploitation."[31] Ultimately, although the Fordist compact improved pay and working conditions for many, it contributed to the decline of militant labour movements, many of which had been socialist oriented and had sought to fundamentally restructure the capitalist system. The decrease in union militancy was clearly evident in Cape Breton where the island's miners—traditionally Canada's most militant workers—engaged in only two general walkouts between 1926 and 1997.[32]

The TLC's adherence to the compact led it and other union groups to advocate participation in government-management-labour conferences. According to historian Charles Lipton, "The problem was that some of the trade union officials who participated in these conferences made harmony with employers and government their prime objective, rather than the winning of results for the workers."[33]

For their part, many corporations eventually recognized unions and exhibited a greater willingness to deal with the new, more moderate leaderships to ensure that workers did not return to their old militant ways, which had proven disruptive to production and had even momentarily challenged the foundations on which capitalism was premised. While class collaboration under the Fordist compact suggested that the workers and the owners had equal voices in this process of industrial legalism, the reality was very different. As historian Gregory Kealey points out:

> The intricate complexity of the legal structures are themselves based on two myths: first, that the two parties involved—capital and labour—meet as equal parties in so-called "free" collective bargaining ("industrial pluralism"); and second, that the state role is simply that of a neutral umpire, aiding the two parties in their deliberations and protecting the interests of the public. The first, of course, perpetuates the commonly-held myth of the equal power of capital and labour, while the second disguises the pro-capitalist role of the state and especially of its potential for coercion.[34]

Nevertheless, the radical union actions of the early 1920s and the repressive reactionary responses of corporations had convinced moderate leaders on both sides that the Fordist compact was preferable to the instability of the past. By the middle of the century, the Fordist compact had become firmly entrenched in Canada. However, as early as 1920, Italian socialist Antonio Gramsci had warned that such compacts should not be the end goal for unions:

> The emergence of an industrial legality is a great victory for the working class, but it is not the ultimate and definitive victory. Industrial legality has improved the working class's standard of living but it is no more than a compromise—a compromise which had to be made and must be supported until the balance of forces favours the working class.[35]

In reality, the Fordist compact did become an acceptable end goal for many unions. Under the compact, Canadian unions made great strides throughout the middle of the 20th century in the areas of wages and working conditions, as well as in the attainment of recognition and universal labour laws. For instance, between 1945 and 1959, average real earnings in the manufacturing sector rose 33 per cent, representing an improvement in the standard of living of many working-class households. These achievements were not solely a result of the Fordist compact, as low levels of unemployment, particularly during the 1940s and 1950s, provided workers with greater leverage at the bargaining table.[36]

As well, the emergence of the Antigonish Movement in eastern Nova Scotia helped improve living conditions for many in Cape Breton and the rest of the Maritimes. While the movement sought to change the economic structures on the community level, it did not include a national or international political project to overthrow the capitalist system. According to sociologist Constance deRoche, "Indeed, the Christian social-democratic Antigonish Movement arose, in part, from the threat of 'godless communism' that was making inroads into local consciousness."[37] Consequently, when it appeared in the late 1920s, its political objectives were less radical than those of the recently deposed militant union leaders as it sought to help rural communities to organize cooperatively—not to overthrow the capitalist system, but to better compete in the larger market. According to its advocates, it represented a "middle way" between laissez-faire capitalism and state socialism.[38] The Antigonish Movement, under the guidance of Father Moses Coady, helped rural communities establish credit unions, co-operative stores and housing. By the end of the 1930s, it had already helped establish 142 credit unions,

39 consumer cooperatives, 11 fish plants and 17 lobster canneries throughout Nova Scotia.[39] The movement also helped miners and steelworkers in industrial Cape Breton to escape their dependence on company housing and company stores and gave many workers access to credit for the first time. The Antigonish Movement's ideas soon spread throughout the Maritimes, across Canada and, eventually, to many countries in the developing world.

As a result of unions operating under the Fordist compact and communities organizing under the principles of the Antigonish Movement, many workers in Cape Breton and elsewhere saw a rise in their standards of living and increased control over their lives. Perhaps most important, however, these advances occurred in the broader context of the Keynesian policy framework, or what has been called the "welfare state." British economist John Maynard Keynes believed that unregulated capitalism was largely responsible for the Great Depression of the 1930s. To address this problem, he advocated government intervention in the economy, particularly in times of recession. However, Keynes was by no means a socialist. In fact, he was a staunch believer in the market system; he just thought that it had to be properly managed in order to limit the suffering during economic downturns, such as the Great Depression.

Near the end of the Second World War, representatives from the allied capitalist nations met in Bretton Woods, New Hampshire, to establish rules for governing the global capitalist economy in the postwar era and to determine how to avoid a repeat of the Great Depression endured by capitalist nations, which had led many to question the viability of the free-market model. Consequently, at Bretton Woods, the United States encountered opposition to its call to implement a global free trade economy for capitalist nations. One of the principal critics of the U.S. proposal was Keynes, the British government's representative at the conference.

Keynes's call for protectionist policies won out over Washington's desire to immediately implement a global free trade system. Keynes called for the acceptance of trade barriers, such as subsidies, tariffs and import quotas, which could then be eliminated slowly over the ensuing decades when the nascent industries of poorer nations had developed to the point where they could compete in a free market. The British economist was basically suggesting that newly industrializing nations of the developing world be permitted to follow the same development path that the United States had taken half-a-century earlier—and was still taking. The U.S. was forced to back down not only on its attempt to allow the free movement of goods across borders but also on permitting the free flow of capital and profits. In essence, Keynesian initiatives sought to moderate capitalist excesses, but they were never intended to challenge the fundamental structures of capitalism. In fact, although the Keynesian policy framework diminished inequality on both the national and international levels, it still maintained the essential structures on which capitalist elites relied to generate wealth.

The Fordist compact between the capitalist owners and the workers was implemented in the global context of Keynesian policies of protectionism and the restricted movement of capital and profits. It was under this policy framework, and in the shadow of the Great Depression, that the welfare state came into being in Canada. In 1940, the Canadian government introduced the country's unemployment insurance program, which was co-funded by workers and the government. Later in the 1940s, the nation's first public housing project was established in Regent Park, Toronto. The country's universal healthcare system was implemented in the 1960s and social assistance programs for the poor came into being during the same decade. Canadian workers had made significant progress not only in wages, working conditions and the right to organize, but also in the provision of social programs by federal and provincial governments. By the late 1950s, under the Keynesian policy framework and the Fordist compact, a significant shift in wealth distribution had occurred as the top 5 per cent of Canada's income earners saw their share of the national income decline to 24 per cent—down from 40 per cent two decades earlier.[40] Even workers in Cape Breton—where there remained a lack of job stability in the steel and coal mining industries during the Keynesian era—enjoyed higher wages and better conditions while those who were laid off benefited from the social safety net.

While there were gains made both in the workplace and with social programs, little or no headway was made on behalf of workers on the political front during these decades. Organized labour primarily endorsed the Co-operative Commonwealth Federation (CCF) party and later the New Democratic Party (NDP) in a national political landscape dominated by the Conservatives and

Liberals. Despite some of the language in the Regina Manifesto, the CCF and the NDP were never truly anti-capitalist as they advocated platforms far more moderate than the revolutionary ideals propagated by the Communist Party and earlier socialist parties such as the Independent Labour Party. According to Lipton, one of the reasons for organized labour's political moderation was the TLC's affiliation with the U.S.-based American Federation of Labor (AFL), which maintained an official policy of neutrality with regard to politics.[41] It called for the AFL and its affiliates to refrain from interfering in political issues not directly related to the workplace. In reality, it had no such neutrality, as the AFL often supported U.S.-government policies seeking to combat the spread of communism, both at home and abroad. As for anti-communism in the TLC, the federation supported the Korean War and, despite the fact that the Communist Party was legal in Canada, adopted a motion at its 1949 convention declaring that "no known communist shall be permitted to hold office in the TLC, provincial federations and central bodies, nor be permitted to sit on any committee of the convention."[42]

By the 1950s, through their acceptance of the Fordist compact and their anti-communist stance, many unions had not merely shifted their political priorities away from class conflict and toward class collaboration, but had actually become defenders of capitalism.[43] However, although workers had accepted the Fordist compact, the capitalist elites were never fully committed to the compromise. When profit margins began to shrink in many industries in the late 1960s and early 1970s, corporations quickly sought ways to reduce production costs. Consequently, it was the owners, not the workers, who eventually broke the compact. Some fifty years after the 1923 Sydney steelworkers' strike and other militant actions of that era, the owners began to dismantle the Fordist compact in order to shift the balance of power, not in favour of the working class as Gramsci had hoped for, but once again to the benefit of the capitalist elites. This shift in class dynamic occurred within the framework of neoliberal globalization.

Dismantling the Compact

When the profit crunch hit in the late 1960s and early 1970s, corporate efforts to reduce their production overhead inevitably led them to focus on labour costs in the industrialized nations of the global North. As political scientist Thom Workman notes, "The Fordist labour regime stood in the way of downward wage reform. [So] the minions of capital have been determined to roll back the Fordist labour regime and open the class compact in the North in order to establish a *modus vivendi* more favourable to capital."[44]

At this time, many economic departments in prestigious North American universities began teaching the doctrine of neoliberalism. Principal among these was the University of Chicago where Milton Friedman became a leading advocate for dismantling the Keynesian policy framework and returning to the classical liberalism of the 19th century. In other words, he sought to restructure the political, social and economic system to dramatically reduce government interference in the economy and thereby achieve a more laissez-faire capitalist system on a global scale.

Neoliberals called for fiscal discipline on the part of governments, which inevitably meant cutbacks in funding for social programs. They also demanded a dismantling of the protectionist system through deregulation and the elimination of subsidies, tariffs and import quotas, as well as of other trade barriers. Neoliberal discourse advocated the removal of restrictions on the free flow of capital and profits, in order to increase foreign investment, and required that national governments privatize state-owned companies because they represented state intervention in the economy and because the private sector could, in theory, operate them more efficiently. Critics, however, claimed that privatizing state-owned companies would threaten the public's access to many services considered essential under the Keynesian policy framework, because the primary objective of private corporations was not to ensure the provision of public services for the entirety of a population, but to maximize profits.

When stagflation—slow economic growth, combined with high inflation—struck Britain and the United States in the 1960s and 1970s, neoliberals saw an opportunity to discredit Keynes' theories and to begin dismantling the Fordist compact. They blamed government intervention for stagflation and called for increased deregulation of the global capitalist economy. The catch phrases of neoliberalism were "efficiency," "growth" and "free trade." Proponents argued that the private sector could run the economy more efficiently than governments and could achieve greater economic growth in a free trade environment. According to neoliberal theory, capitalist elites would reinvest the wealth generated by economic growth to generate even more growth and the benefits would trickle down to all sectors of society.

In September 1973, the South American country of Chile became the testing ground for the neoliberal doctrine, following the overthrow of the democratically elected socialist government of President Salvador Allende. The U.S.-backed dictator, General Augusto Pinochet, placed a group of Chilean economists who had studied under Friedman—known as "the Chicago Boys"—in charge of dismantling the social and economic programs implemented by Allende. They set about restructuring the country's economy in accordance with neoliberal doctrine. By the late 1980s, U.S.-dominated international financial institutions such as the International Monetary Fund (IMF) and the World Bank were imposing neoliberalism on most Latin American nations. Following the end of the Cold War, neoliberalism was implemented not only throughout the global South but also in the former Soviet republics.

During the 1980s, neoliberalism was implemented not only in the impoverished nations of Latin America, but also in Britain by the Conservative government of Margaret Thatcher and in the United States by Republican President Ronald Reagan. Following the Canadian Conservative party's victory at the polls in 1984, Canada's Prime Minister Brian Mulroney announced that "Canada was open for business again" and quickly followed in the footsteps of Thatcher and Reagan. Over the next twenty years, Conservative and Liberal governments implemented neoliberal policies that established favourable economic conditions for multinational corporations through privatizations, reductions in corporate income taxes, the restructuring of social programs and the dismantling of the protectionist system. Free-market policies implemented at home and abroad allowed companies to dismantle the Fordist compact by shifting production to the global South where they could exploit cheaper labour and natural resources. The implementation of NAFTA in 1994 was part of this neoliberal process.

Mulroney first introduced privatization as a policy in his government's 1985 budget. Over the next twenty years, thirty Crown corporations were privatized including Petro-Canada, Air Canada, Canadian National Railways and numerous telecommunications companies.[45] The privatization of Petro-Canada, which was initiated under Mulroney in 1990 and finally completed by the Liberal government of Paul Martin in 2004, resulted in 40 per cent of the company's workforce losing their jobs by 1995.[46] While the company did become more competitive and efficient under private-sector ownership, rarely did anyone ask the question: Who were the beneficiaries of the new efficiency? After all, profits from Petro-Canada did not go into the government's coffers to help fund social programs such as healthcare and education, but benefited a relatively small group of corporate executives and shareholders. Furthermore, the privatization of Petro-Canada, along with the dismantling of the National Energy Program, contributed to undermining Canada's energy security as foreign corporations gained greater control over the country's oil reserves and Canadians became increasingly subject to the whims of the global oil market, affecting the cost of gasoline and heating oil among other things. While neoliberals operated on the assumption that economic growth benefited all, it soon became apparent that the streamlining of these newly privatized companies in order to make them more profitable meant that thousands of Canadians would lose decent-paying jobs.

It wasn't merely Crown corporations that fell victim to neoliberalism, the country's social safety net was also hit. In 1990, the government stopped paying into the country's unemployment insurance program—renamed Employment Insurance (EI) in 1996—leaving the onus on workers to fund it. Then, in the ensuing years, Ottawa established stricter eligibility requirements and reduced the length of time that unemployment insurance could be collected. According to a May 2007 Statistics Canada report on income distribution:

> The generosity of the EI program has steadily eroded since the 1970s, due to successive reductions in benefit levels and tightening of eligibility requirements. One indicator of EI generosity is the beneficiaries-to-unemployed ratio (BU ratio) which fell from 82.9% in 1990 to 43.9% in 2004.[47]

Gibbs and Leech

The principle benefit to corporations of EI restructuring was the establishment of a surplus pool of cheap labour, as the unemployed had to re-enter the job market sooner than they previously would have. This inevitably created more competition for existing jobs and drove down wages in many sectors. As political scientist Keith Banting points out, "Virtually every program with more direct implications for labour market performance has been restructured in important ways, reducing the levels of economic security provided to beneficiaries."[48]

The changes in the unemployment insurance program also resulted in annual surpluses in the billions of dollars by the late 1990s, as the share of unemployment premiums paid by workers had not been reduced to the same degree that benefits had been. The massive surpluses were then transferred from the unemployment insurance program to the government's general budget. In effect, the restructuring of the unemployment insurance program shifted a greater share of the tax burden to individuals because a percentage of the unemployment premiums paid by workers was going toward the government's general revenues. Meanwhile, Conservative and Liberal governments were reducing corporate income tax rates. The Chrétien and Martin governments incrementally lowered the corporate income tax rate from 29 per cent in the late 1990s to 21 per cent by 2005.[49] In 2006, the Conservative government of Stephen Harper announced that the corporate tax rate would be further reduced to 18.5 per cent by 2011.[50]

Another controversial tax reform that benefited corporations was the Mulroney government's introduction of the GST to replace the manufacturers' sales tax (MST). Because companies no longer had to pay the MST, the reform shifted a greater share of the tax burden to individual Canadians, who bore the burden of the newly implemented GST. The Canadian Council of Chief Executives (CCCE), the leading advocate of Canada's largest 150 corporations, was one of the principal lobbyists for the elimination of the MST. In fact, the CCCE's influential role in most aspects of the federal government's implementation of neoliberalism, including NAFTA and the proposed post-9/11 Security and Prosperity Partnership of North America, highlights the ongoing alliance between the federal government and Canada's economic elites. The CCCE is unabashedly pro-neoliberal and openly brags about its influence:

Over the past three decades, the Council has played a private sector leadership role in shaping fiscal, taxation, trade, competition, energy, environmental, education and corporate governance policies. We have been groundbreakers in advancing Canada's competitiveness agenda and our mandate and work encompasses North American and global issues. We have been referred to as the world's most effective CEO-based organization dedicated to public policy development and solutions.[51]

Maude Barlow, the national chairperson of the Council of Canadians, Canada's largest public advocacy organization, agrees that the CCCE has indeed been very influential in convincing the Canadian government to implement neoliberalism. In fact, says Barlow, the Canadian government "is listening almost exclusively to the Canadian Council of Chief Executives and its think-tank allies." But as she makes clear, "The Canadian Council of Chief Executives does not speak for Canada. It speaks for the interests of its members, many of which are branch plants of American corporations."[52]

The federal government's neoliberal policies have benefited corporations at the expense of the social welfare of Canadians. Ottawa's promotion of a policy of decentralization has shifted more of the burden for managing social programs to provincial governments. However, there has been no corresponding shift in funding from Ottawa to help provincial governments handle the additional responsibilities. As a result, many provincial governments have had little choice but to follow Ottawa down the path of austerity because they lack essential revenues.

Both the private and public sectors disguise the fact that the rise of neoliberalism has been a conscious, ideologically driven policy decision, presenting it as evolutionary and inevitable. Consequently, as sociologist Constance deRoche points out:

> Both private and public sectors now abjure responsibility for a Fordist political economy from which they once benefited and in whose design they participated. Today, neither sector accepts the obligation to create jobs, and governments point to fiscal crises that impede efforts at redistribution. Corporations downsize and outsource, while governments download economic and social responsibilities onto communities, citizens, and "third sector" organizations that rely heavily on unpaid labour. Both sectors have been actively promoting a neo-liberal orthodoxy that legitimates corporate libertarianism and government impotency.[53]

The Era of Industrial Decline

In Cape Breton, the implementation of neoliberalism proved particularly devastating for workers. For much of the 20th century the Sydney steel plant and the surrounding coal mines were the island's primary economic mainstays. In 1930, BESCO was restructured and became the Dominion Steel and Coal Corporation (DOSCO). In the ensuing decades, the steel plant struggled to remain profitable because of its geographic remoteness from the heart of industrial Canada and the poor quality of Cape Breton's high-sulphur coal. The company tried to address the latter issue in the late 1950s by importing low-sulphur coal from the United States to mix with Cape Breton coal. While this strategy did help improve the quality of the steel, it also diminished the demand for Cape Breton coal; five mines were closed in 1960. In the mid-1960s, DOSCO put its financially troubled steel plant and coal mines up for sale and, with no private-sector takers, the federal government decided to establish a Crown corporation called the Cape Breton Development Corporation (DEVCO) to take over ownership of the mines in 1967. The original plan was to keep the mines operating for the next fifteen years while restructuring Cape Breton's economy to diminish its reliance on the coal industry. The last mine did not close, however, until 2001. During the same period, the Nova Scotia provincial government established the Sydney Steel Corporation (SYSCO) to take over the steel plant, which it operated for the next thirty-four years, before finally shutting it down in 2001.

In the eyes of neoliberals, Cape Breton's steel plant and coal mines were quintessential examples of the failure of Keynesian policies: government ownership and operation of money-losing, debt-ridden industries serving little public good beyond providing jobs for a few thousand workers. In reality, the economic problem related to the viability of Cape Breton's steel and coal industries was not caused by Keynesian policies. In fact, Keynesian policies, both before and after the government takeover of the steel plant and coal mines, had helped alleviate the hardships caused by the industrialization process that occurred under a more laissez-faire capitalist model. To be more precise, the problem was actually caused by government support for capitalist ownership of the steel plant and coal mines in the name of industrialization back at the beginning of the

20th century. At that time, the plant and mines served the economic interests only of the owners; it wasn't until the Keynesian era that workers began earning a living wage.

The deindustrialization and mass layoffs that occurred in Cape Breton under neoliberalism cannot simply be blamed on the financial failings and unfeasibility of the steel plant and coal mines. A look at how the federal government's neoliberal policies affected profitable steel operations in other regions of Canada illustrates that profitability did not translate into job security for workers. As a result of Keynesian protectionist policies, Canada's steel industry had become internationally competitive by the 1960s. Also, tariffs placed on imports allowed Canada to dramatically diminish its dependence on imported steel between the 1940s and 1970s.[54] Within a decade of the implementation of neoliberalism in Canada, however, the steel industry would experience a dramatic reversal. According to an Industry Canada report published in 2000, the country had become a net importer of steel by 1994 after being a net exporter only a decade earlier.[55] Imports from such countries as Japan, Russia, South Korea, Brazil and Mexico were supplying an increasing percentage of the domestic market, reaching 40 per cent in 1998—almost double their market share only eight years earlier. During the same period, employment in the domestic steel industry plummeted by 19 per cent as more than 7,000 workers lost their jobs.[56]

The deep entrenchment of the neoliberal doctrine in official circles is evident in the aforementioned Industry Canada report. Despite the significant job losses in the steel industry and in other manufacturing sectors that resulted from the federal government's neoliberal policies, the report notes that "[i]n the WTO [World Trade Organization], Canada is still looking forward to further liberalization of trade through various negotiating processes." The report goes on to point out that the "Canadian primary steel industry has demonstrated a significant openness on the international market since 1990" and that under "Canada's general trade policies there are no quotas, import restrictions or non-tariff barriers to steel imports into the Canadian market save those sanctioned by the WTO."[57] The report then notes that, given "the continuing expansion of global steel production in developing countries and the high percentage of global steel production that is traded internationally, Canadian steelmakers are likely to face even more import competition in the future." The report concludes by suggesting that Canadian steel producers should respond to increasing imports by taking a neoliberal approach by providing "higher value added products and emphasizing service, delivery and competitive prices," the latter undoubtedly requiring a reduction in labour costs.[58]

The Algoma Steel Plant in the Ontario town of Sault Ste. Marie was a profitable operation during the Keynesian era and in the mid-1980s employed some twelve thousand workers. The implementation of neoliberalism over the next decade proved devastating, however, for the plant's profitability and its workforce. The government's dismantling of protectionist measures meant that Algoma struggled to compete with imported steel, much of which was manufactured by subsidized Japanese companies or through the use of cheap labour in the global South. The company went into bankruptcy protection twice during the 1990s, before finally becoming competitive due to technological advancements and a massive downsizing of its workforce. In 2002, the company only employed some three thousand steelworkers, having laid off close to 75 per cent of its workforce over the previous decade.[59]

Steelworkers have not been the only ones hurt by the Canadian government's implementation of neoliberal policies. While the automobile industry was making substantial profits during the first decade following the implementation of NAFTA, it was simultaneously laying off some fifteen thousand Canadian workers.[60] The companies were taking advantage of NAFTA by relocating operations to Mexico, in order to exploit the cheap labour available in that country. Meanwhile, the new auto industry jobs created in Canada tended to be non-unionized, as with the Toyota and Honda assembly plants in the Ontario towns of Cambridge and Alliston respectively.[61]

In the end, it was not simply the failure of the Sydney steel plant to generate profits that led to its closing. Even if the Sydney plant had been profitable, the implementation of neoliberalism would have led to the laying off of workers, as the cases of the Algoma Steel Plant and the auto industry—both of which achieved profitability under the Keynesian policy framework—make clear. Ultimately, the dismantling of the Fordist compact was not about unloading unprofitable manufacturing operations like the Sydney steel plant, it was about increasing the profits of many already profitable corporations at the expense of Canadian workers.

In reality, it never made economic sense to establish large steel and coal-mining industries in Cape Breton as the struggle to achieve profitability over the 20th century made evident. As a result of this industrialization process, the population of industrial Cape Breton—and of Sydney in particular—increased dramatically, fuelled by an unsustainable economic model. Because of this it has proven difficult to find economic alternatives to steel and coal in what, following the closure of the steel plant and the last coal mine, must be considered an overpopulated rural region. Ultimately, Cape Breton was an experiment in industrialization that went wrong, not because of Keynesian policies, but because of unbridled, government-backed capitalist greed.

The legacy of Cape Breton's century-long experiment in industrial capitalism consists not only of high unemployment and economic insecurity, but also a serious health crisis and environmental devastation. For decades, industrial Cape Breton has endured the highest rates of cancer and heart disease in Canada.[62] This tragic reality is not surprising when one considers that almost one hundred years of industrial pollutants from the steel plant created Canada's largest toxic waste site: the Sydney Tar Ponds, a cesspool containing 700,000 tons of toxic sludge. While diet and lifestyle also contribute to health problems, many Cape Bretoners have been directly affected by industrial pollution. In 1998, for example, seventeen families were forced to abandon their homes on Frederick Street, which is situated adjacent to the Tar Ponds, their houses subsequently demolished. The residents were displaced because the toxic waste had penetrated their homes and their bodies:

> Kidney infections, nosebleeds, nausea, diarrhea, headaches, tingling joints, ear infections, bloody stools, bloody urine and severe coughs were sweeping through the families that lived in the 17 homes of Frederick Street. All the dogs had died, one after it literally glowed in the dark. Deformed mice, with bat-like heads and kangaroo-like feet, had appeared. Lilacs and roses had bloomed pitch black and then disintegrated. One day in early May, when Debbie Ouellette was cleaning up her backyard, she noticed a bright yellow goo seeping out of the embankment directly behind her house and fluorescent orange chemicals lighting up the creek that runs through her property.[63]

While the process of cleaning up the Tar Ponds is now being portrayed as an economic opportunity, Cape Breton faces another environmental problem, this time related to the coal mining sector—a problem resulting from Nova Scotia's utility company, Nova Scotia Power (NSP), being overly dependent on coal for electricity generation. At the beginning of the 21st century, 76 per cent of NSP's electricity production was being generated by coal-burning power plants—three located in Cape Breton.[64] The environmental consequences of burning this coal have been devastating. Not only does the dirtiest of the fossil fuels emit pollutants such as sulphur dioxides, nitrogen oxides and mercury affecting people living in the immediate vicinity of power plants, it is the most significant contributor to global climate change, through its emission of greenhouse gases such as carbon dioxide (CO_2).

NSP itself became a symbol of neoliberalism when the Conservative government of Donald Cameron sold the provincially owned utility in 1992 in what was, at the time, Canada's largest privatization. The newly privatized utility company ensured that Cape Breton's last coal mine would be shut down, not because NSP intended to dramatically increase its use of cleaner renewable sources of energy such as solar, wind or tidal, but rather to take advantage of the new global economy—including coal from Colombia.

Back to the Future

For more than a century, capitalist elites have sought to preserve an economic order ensuring the accumulation of profits. In the early decades of industrialization in Canada, political and economic elites formed an alliance in order to repress any workers who dared to demand even a reasonable share of the wealth resulting from their labour. Nowhere was the conflict between owners and workers more evident than in Cape Breton. By the mid-1920s, however, the capitalist elites had succeeded in defeating the threat posed by Cape Breton's radical unions. The ensuing Fordist compact, along with the establishment of the Keynesian policy framework, finally allowed many workers to modestly improve their standard of living, although it failed to achieve any significant progress toward equality. Meanwhile, the workers' failure to achieve greater political power ultimately rendered them impotent when capitalist elites set about establishing the necessary conditions to implement neoliberalism. The dismantling of the Keynesian policy framework—in both the North and the South—subsequently allowed corporations to move their operations to virtually anywhere in the world in order to increase profits by exploiting cheap labour.

From its inception, capitalism has depended on access to cheap labour and natural resources located in the global South. For hundreds of years, the European colonial powers relied on the raw materials they extracted from their colonies to fuel Europe's industrial development. The same European nations, along with the United States, Japan, Australia and Canada, remained dominant in the 20th century and ensured that neocolonial international institutions such as the IMF and the World Bank would facilitate the continued exploitation of the global South—although Keynesian-influenced protectionism somewhat limited the degree of that exploitation. But with the dismantling of the Keynesian policy framework and the emergence of neoliberalism, the global North has seen a significant diminishing of workers' rights, and people in the global South have endured a deepening of the neocolonial process of exploitation.

The neoliberal restructuring of Colombia's economy ensured that the country's valuable natural resources, particularly oil and coal, were made available to multinational corporations seeking to dismantle the Fordist compact. The exploitation of cheap labour in Colombia has allowed multinational mining companies to increase profits by producing and exporting Colombian coal to Cape Breton and other parts of eastern Canada, as well as the United States and Europe. Tragically, extracting coal and other natural resources in Colombia has often been directly linked to gross violations of human rights, perpetrated against communities and workers. Consequently, the latter have found themselves in a struggle eerily reminiscent of the one waged by Cape Breton's miners and steelworkers almost a century ago.

Two

Colombia in the Era of Neoliberal Globalization

Three months after the last coal mine in Cape Breton was closed down, two hundred soldiers, police and private security personnel forcibly displaced residents from the small Afro-Colombian town of Tabaco in northeastern Colombia. As bulldozers flattened their houses, church and school, stunned media representatives caught the destruction on film, while community leaders denounced the invasion. More than seven hundred people were forcibly displaced to allow for the expansion of the world's largest open-pit coal mine, El Cerrejón. Neoliberal reforms implemented in Colombia had made the coal extracted from the Cerrejón mine available on favourable terms to multinational mining companies for export, not only to Cape Breton, but also to the United States and Europe.

In the meantime, while communities such as Tabaco have been violently displaced by multinational corporations seeking to exploit the country's natural resources, Colombian workers have been risking their lives to fight for better wages and working conditions. Because union leaders engage in a struggle to improve the life of Colombia's workers, the government, the military and right-wing paramilitaries assume them to be leftist guerrillas. For the past twenty years, Colombia has been, by far, the most dangerous country in the world for those who fight for workers' rights. In fact, almost 75 per cent of the union leaders killed worldwide during the previous two decades were Colombian. The paramilitaries, with the help of the U.S.-backed Colombian military, have with virtual impunity waged a "dirty war" against Colombia's unions. Consequently, Colombia's workers have endured even greater levels of violence and repression than those experienced by Cape Breton's steelworkers and miners a century ago.

The Path to Neoliberalism

Throughout the middle of the 20th century, many nations in the global South implemented Keynesian protectionist policies to facilitate industrialization. Import substitution industrialization (ISI) policies were intended to protect nascent domestic industries so that countries in the global South could become industrial nations rather than simply exporters of raw materials and importers of manufactured goods. In essence, they were following the same development path as that previously taken by the U.S. and Canada. Despite the prevalence of repressive dictatorships, many countries, particularly in Latin America and Asia, made their greatest advances during the ISI period in reducing poverty and infant mortality rates and in raising average levels of education and standards of living. In short, the Keynesian policy framework improved the lot of millions in the global South, albeit to a much lesser degree than it helped workers in Canada and other nations in the North. However, as with Keynesian policies in the North, the ISI model was never intended to challenge the capitalist structures, only to create a more equitable distribution of wealth.

As occurred in Canada and other nations of the North during the Keynesian era, domestic and foreign capitalist elites in the South tolerated the ISI model, but only to undermine radical elements inspired in part by the Soviet socialist model, particularly in the aftermath of the Great Depression. During this time, as part of its Cold War strategy to combat communist influence worldwide, the U.S. government encouraged private banks, as well as U.S.-dominated international financial institutions such as the IMF and the World Bank, to provide loans to dictatorships and quasi-democratic regimes in pro-capitalist nations of the South. The money only partly benefited local populations, because much of it flowed into the pockets of the corrupt political and economic elites who would ensure that their nations remained staunchly anti-communist. Ultimately, irresponsible lending by Western banks and irresponsible borrowing by non-democratic regimes allied with the capitalist nations of the global North led to many countries becoming mired in a severe debt crisis by the early 1980s.

The IMF used the debt crisis in the global South as a conduit for imposing neoliberalism on economically and fiscally troubled nations. In return for desperately needed bailout loans, borrowing nations were required to implement neoliberal policies demanding debtor nations privatize state-owned companies, reduce social spending, and eliminate trade and investment barriers, which opened up their cheap labour, natural resources and markets to multinational corporations based in the North. Unlike most other Latin American nations, however, Colombia avoided the debt crisis of the 1980s and did not succumb to neoliberal globalization until the following decade.

To understand the economic trajectory of Colombia, it is instructive to explore both what is unique about the country's history and what aspects of its economic development reflect regional trends. Colombia's history, like that of other countries in the region, is dotted with attempts at broad-based redistributive experiments, such as the labour and agrarian reforms of the 1930s. While militant labour, mostly represented by the Colombian Communist Party, never gained widespread backing, it did achieve a number of victories throughout the 20th century and has had consistent support in some regions of the country to this day.[1]

While managing or suppressing these popular calls for reform, Colombia's nationally oriented capitalist elites remained relatively united in their maintenance of a nationally focused economic model throughout the Cold War era. Under the Keynesian policy framework, Colombia implemented ISI policies that sought to utilize protectionist measures to help the nation industrialize and to diminish the economy's reliance on the export of natural resources. In other words, the objective of the industrialization process was to move Colombia away from the periphery of the global capitalist economy and closer to its centre—not unlike the goals of the industrialization process that occurred in Canada at the beginning of the 20th century.

In 1958, Colombia's two dominant political parties, the Liberals and Conservatives, initiated a power-sharing pact known as the National Front. The establishment of the National Front government ended a decade of civil conflict—known simply as *La Violencia*,

The Violence—which had been waged between supporters of the country's two traditional parties. The power-sharing pact ensured that capitalist development took place in an environment with the overall consensus of the elite on the direction of the economy. As political scientist Carlos E. Juarez notes:

> A key feature of the National Front period was that major producer and employer associations, representing dominant and allied class interests, enjoyed privileged access to the *policy* process while subordinate classes (the peasantry, workers and the urban poor) had little or none.[2]

Despite the fact that the National Front officially ceased to exist in 1974, this arrangement continues today with the country's dominant elites—representing the transnationally oriented and U.S.-friendly capitalist elites under neoliberalism—being overrepresented in policy-making circles while the poor majority remain largely invisible.

The careful management of the economy during the ISI decades meant that, unlike other countries in the region, Colombia did not find itself excessively indebted to international lenders. As a result, the widespread implementation of neoliberalism in Colombia did not occur until the 1990s. The dismantling of the ISI model and the rise of neoliberalism—and the corresponding policy shift to prioritize transnational economic interests over national economic interests—occurred as a result, at least in part, of the Colombian government's need for U.S. aid to combat the cocaine cartels. In the fall of 1989, U.S. President George Bush announced the $2.2 billion Andean Initiative, which he declared would "encourage and support fundamental economic reform in the countries of the region on the basis of market-driven policies."[3] Colombian President César Gaviria initiated *la apertura*—the Opening—of the Colombian economy the following year, paving the way for the dismantling of the ISI model and an increase in foreign investment.

At the same time that the Bush administration was calling on Colombia to dismantle its Keynesian protectionist policies and to open up its economy to foreign corporations, another neoliberal decision made by the U.S. government would seriously undermine Colombia's traditionally stable coffee economy. For many years, the cultivation of coffee beans had provided farmers in the coffee-growing regions with a measure of security and stability in the midst of Colombia's violence. However, the international market price for coffee—Colombia's leading legal export for most of the 20th century—plummeted in the post-Cold War era, forcing many farmers to seek alternative means of survival. Consequently, increasing numbers of farmers began replacing their coffee bushes with coca plants, the leaves of which provide the key ingredient in cocaine.

The dilemma faced by Colombia's coffee growers began with the 1989 dismantling of the International Coffee Agreement (ICA) by the United States. The ICA was a Keynesian-influenced pact that ensured a degree of equality in the power dynamics between poor producing countries and rich consuming nations by establishing a price range for coffee guaranteeing growers a minimum of $1.20 per pound. With the Soviet Union and the corresponding communist threat collapsing, and the capitalist elites in the United States pushing for the dismantling of the Keynesian policy framework, the U.S. government backed out of the agreement. Because the United States was by far the world's largest consumer of coffee, its withdrawal from the ICA rendered the pact null and void.

The end of the ICA meant that the global price of coffee would henceforth be determined by supply and demand. The World Bank then quickly manipulated the delicate balance between supply and demand by promoting a development project in Vietnam during the 1990s that encouraged that country's farmers to grow coffee. The program was so "successful" that Vietnamese production surpassed Colombia's in 2001 and the country became the second-largest producer of coffee after Brazil. However, a resulting global glut in coffee caused the market price to plummet from more than $2 a pound when the ICA was dismantled at the end of the 1980s to 58 cents by the end of 2001. Consequently, coffee growers around the world, including those in Vietnam, were desperately struggling to survive by cultivating a crop that sold for less than it cost to produce.

The declining cost of coffee, meanwhile, was not reflected at the retail end of the equation. The multinational coffee corporations reaped the benefits of the dismantling of the ICA and the World Bank's Vietnam project. By keeping retail prices relatively constant while the cost of coffee beans plummeted, corporations increased their earnings dramatically. In fact, in 2001, the same year that Vietnam's production surpassed Colombia's and the global price for coffee beans hit rock bottom, U.S.-based Starbucks reported a record profit of $181.2 million—a 92 per cent increase over the previous year.[4]

In 1999, after almost a decade of neoliberalism, the Colombian economy sank into its worst recession since the Great Depression, more than half a century earlier. The official unemployment rate soared to 22 per cent and, according to the World Bank, the poverty level increased from 60 per cent to 64 per cent of the population during the second half of the 1990s.[5] It had taken longer than most other Latin American countries, but Colombia had finally reached the point of fiscal and economic desperation that forced it to turn to the IMF for a bailout loan. The IMF then used its newly gained leverage to pressure Colombia into further liberalizing its economy.

Plan Colombia and U.S. Intervention

In the 1960s, many Colombians had responded to the National Front government by taking up arms and forming several leftist guerrilla groups. The country's largest rebel group, the Revolutionary Armed Forces of Colombia (Fuerzas Armades Revolucionarias de Colombia, FARC), has been battling the U.S.-backed government for more than forty years. The FARC is seeking to establish a socialist state to redistribute wealth in a country where 85 per cent of the rural population lives in poverty.[6] Colombia's capitalist elites have responded to the guerrilla threat by forming right-wing paramilitary groups that work hand-in-glove with the Colombian military. The paramilitaries have been the principal perpetrators of the dirty war waged against anyone perceived to be a leftist. As a result, unionists, human rights workers, community leaders, teachers and anyone else advocating political or social change has become a victim of massacres, forced displacement or disappearance. According to one of Colombia's leading human rights lawyers, Alirio Uribe of the José Alvear Restrepo Lawyers' Collective:

> Historically, the paramilitaries represented the privatization of the dirty war. The government created these dark forces to carry out the repression, to kill civilians, journalists and others, and then the State could say that it has nothing to do with it because the paramilitaries are responsible. But the paramilitaries have never been independent from the State. They have never fought against

the State. They have always been allied with the civil authorities, the public forces, the army and the police, with all the security organizations of the State.[7]

At the end of the 20th century, despite the fact that the paramilitaries were Colombia's principal drug traffickers and violators of human rights, the U.S. war on drugs sought to target the FARC. While the rebel group was not engaged in the production or trafficking of cocaine, it did profit from the taxes it imposed on coca-growing plantations and cocaine-processing labs located in rebel-controlled territory. However, it was not the FARC's involvement in the drug trade that concerned Washington so much as the rebel group's growing military strength and the increasing threat it posed to U.S. economic interests in Colombia. In 1999, U.S. Secretary of Energy Bill Richardson visited the Colombian city of Cartagena to secure U.S. economic interests in the South American nation. During his visit, Richardson announced that "[t]he United States and its allies will invest millions of dollars in two areas of the Colombian economy, in the areas of mining and energy, and to secure these investments we are tripling military aid to Colombia."[8]

The following year, it became apparent that the U.S. government intended to use its war on drugs as a conduit for militarily implementing neoliberalism in Colombia. The Clinton administration announced the launching of a five-year, multi-billion dollar counter-narcotics initiative called Plan Colombia. Clearly, Plan Colombia constituted the military component of the strategy outlined by Richardson in Cartagena. Military aid constituted more than 70 per cent of Plan Colombia's funding, making Colombia the third-largest recipient of U.S. military aid after Israel and Egypt. The three principal objectives of the Plan were to reduce the amount of coca cultivated in Colombia over the next five years by 50 per cent, to end the country's civil conflict, primarily by targeting coca crops in FARC-controlled territory in order to undermine the rebel group's funding, and to boost the country's economy. The latter objective was to be achieved through a $2.7 billion dollar loan agreement that the Colombian government had signed with the IMF the previous year in an effort to overcome its economic crisis. In other words, the IMF loan constituted the economic component of Plan Colombia.

The neoliberal reforms agreed to by Colombia in return for the IMF loan sought to make the extensive mineral and oil resources that Energy Secretary Richardson had referred to available for exploitation by multinational corporations. In essence, the IMF loan would establish the desired economic conditions for multinational energy companies while military aid under Plan Colombia would help provide the necessary security in resource-rich regions of the country, largely controlled by leftist guerrillas.

Under Plan Colombia, the Colombian government's two agendas—security and economic growth—have not been mutually exclusive. Members of civil society who criticized the government's security and economic policies soon found themselves labelled as "subversives" or "terrorists." In 2003, eighty non-governmental organizations (NGOs) issued a report stating that the human rights situation had worsened under President Alvaro Uribe because of "indiscriminate military operations" that sought to achieve "social control and to implant terror in the population." According to the report, these security policies had led to a dramatic increase in the number of people whose human rights were violated by extrajudicial execution, forced disappearance, torture or arbitrary detention during Uribe's first year in office.[9] President Uribe responded to the report by publicly linking the NGOs with the country's leftist guerrillas, saying that "[e]very time a security policy is carried out in Colombia to defeat terrorism, when terrorists start feeling weak, they immediately send their spokesmen to talk about human rights."[10]

Nowhere is the State's repression of its critics more evident than in its targeting of unionists. In 2006, Colombians accounted for 78 of the 144 unionists killed worldwide. According to the International Confederation of Trade Unions (ICFTU), there were 1,165 documented murders of Colombian trade union members between 1994 and 2006. However, the state has convicted the perpetrators in only 14 of these cases—an impunity rate of over 95 per cent.[11] Additionally, neoliberal reforms were a significant contributing factor in the dissolution of more than 195 trade union organizations between 1991 and 2001, resulting in union membership declining by more than 100,000 workers during that period. With less than 5 per cent of the workforce unionized in 2007—compared with 15 per cent twenty years earlier—Colombia has the lowest unionization rate in Latin America.[12]

The IMF-imposed economic reforms played a significant role in undermining public-sector unions in particular, as they called for the privatization of state-owned entities such as banks and utility and mining companies. The privatized companies proved a bonanza for those who could afford to purchase them—multinational corporations and Colombia's economic elite, which is comprised of five large conglomerates dominating the nation's industrial sector and owning virtually all major media outlets.

The privatization process resulted in massive layoffs as investors streamlined operations in order to maximize profits with little regard for the public welfare. Many laid-off workers have been forced to work in the informal sector, mostly as street vendors, where they experience extreme financial insecurity as a result of their functioning outside the system and therefore lack steady income, health benefits and a pension plan. Between 1992 and 2000, the number of Colombians working in the informal economy increased from 55.3 per cent to 61.4 per cent of the workforce.[13]

Under neoliberal globalization, the categories of "labour" have become more complex, particularly with regard to understanding social and economic dislocation and transformation. By carefully constructing a labour paradigm to suit the flexible and decentralized neoliberal economy, the Colombian government has facilitated a process by which huge categories of people have become largely irrelevant to macroeconomic indicators and indeed to democratic decision-making. This class of unorganized labour functioning in the informal economy is often viewed as "disposable." In fact, these workers are only seen as relevant to the degree that their poverty and crime infringes on the lifestyles of the middle and upper classes. Whereas the struggles of organized labour remain crucial in understanding social change in countries of the global South such as Colombia, the precarious existence of this invisible class of informal labourers underscores the neoliberal model's increasingly unjust exclusivity.

Greater social and economic insecurity under neoliberalism is evident not only in the shift from the formal to the informal economy for many workers, but also in the out-migration of Colombians seeking work overseas, particularly in the United States. Many Colombians who are unemployed or struggling to survive in the informal economy have become increasingly dependent on remittances sent home by family members working abroad. In 1999, Colombians living overseas sent $1.7 billion in remittances back home. Five years later, this amount had risen to $3.7 billion, a startling 220 per cent increase.[14] Clearly, neoliberalism was facilitating the exportation not only of Colombia's natural resources, but also of its human ones. Having so many economic refugees fleeing the country's harsh economic reality has devastated the social fabric of both families and communities. In March 2002, even Colombia's labour minister, Angelino Garzón, admitted that the wealth generated under neoliberalism was not trickling down to the majority of Colombians and that the policies of the IMF had "contributed to the impoverishment of large sectors of the population."[15]

There are two principal reasons the Colombian government has been so eager to implement neoliberal policies that have proven so socially and economically devastating for broad sectors of the population. First, many of the country's political leaders have been educated in universities in the global North where they were indoctrinated in neoliberalism. President Alvaro Uribe, for example, studied administration and management at Harvard. And second, the Colombian government, like many others in the global South, must abide by the IMF's stringent demands to implement neoliberal reforms or face a political and economic backlash from international lending institutions, multinational corporations and the governments of the global North, particularly the United States.

In January 2003, Colombia was again forced to turn to the IMF, this time receiving a $2.1 billion loan. To comply with IMF structural adjustment demands, the Colombian government restructured the oil sector, establishing regulations beneficial to multinational companies. In 1999, foreign oil companies were required to sign association contracts with Colombia's state oil company, Ecopetrol, under which each party would own 50 per cent of the oil produced. By 2004, the multinationals no longer had to enter into partnership with Ecopetrol, and they were given the rights to 100 per cent of the oil they produced. During the same period, the Colombian government reduced the royalty rate multinationals paid on each barrel of oil, from 20 per cent to 8 per cent.[16] Despite the favourable terms for foreign oil companies and the diminished financial benefits for Colombia under the new contracts, José Armando Zamora, director of the government's National Hydrocarbon Agency, insisted that the contract concessions "do not represent a loss of sovereignty or the sale of the nation's resources."[17]

While neoliberal reforms had established the economic conditions desired by multinational oil companies, U.S. military aid was intended to provide the necessary security in guerrilla-controlled, resource-rich regions of the country. The Plan Colombia counternarcotics initiative focused on the oil-rich department—or province—of Putumayo, while the Bush administration's war on terror targeted the oil-rich department of Arauca. Consequently, U.S. military intervention in Colombia represents a microcosm of the broader role played by the U.S. military-industrial complex as both an engine for economic growth within the United States and a means of defending the global capitalist system, particularly U.S. corporate interests overseas. In 2007, the U.S. government's military-related budget was a whopping $728.2 billion.[18] A huge portion of this money went to U.S. corporations in the military-industrial complex to manufacture weapons, ammunition, missiles, planes, helicopters and ships, among other military-related equipment. This money also funded military research, maintenance of weaponry and the hiring of dozens of military contractors including Blackwater in Iraq and DynCorp in Colombia. The dual role of the military industrial complex—as an engine of economic growth and a defender of the global capitalist system—illustrates how global capitalism and global conflict are intrinsically linked.

The relationship between U.S. military funding and the economic interests of capitalist elites is clearly evident in Colombia. The initial $1.3 billion aid package for Plan Colombia was mostly distributed to U.S. corporations such as United Technologies ($228 million for Sikorsky Black Hawk helicopters) and Textron ($60 million to upgrade Huey helicopters).[19] Millions of dollars also went to military contractors such as DynCorp, which provided retired military personnel to pilot and maintain the helicopters. During the ensuing years, helicopters and other military hardware provided under Plan Colombia and the war on terror would be used to combat the heavy guerrilla presence in both Putumayo and Arauca, where rebels frequently attacked pipelines and other oil infrastructure belonging to U.S. companies. In 2001, for example, guerrillas demanding that the government nationalize the oil industry bombed Los Angeles-based Occidental Petroleum's oil pipeline in Arauca a record 170 times, shutting it down for 240 days during the year and costing the company $100 million in lost earnings.[20] In response, U.S. Army special forces troops were deployed to Arauca as part of the Bush administration's global war on terror, even though guerrilla attacks in Colombia primarily sought to target the bottom line of U.S. corporations rather than the lives of U.S. citizens.

In both Arauca and Putumayo, the Colombian army's principal objective has not been to defend a civilian population caught in the midst of an armed conflict, but to protect foreign companies taking advantage of neoliberal reforms. As the Colombian army's Lieutenant Colonel Francisco Javier Cruz, commander of twelve hundred troops in Putumayo, made clear in 2004, "Security is the most important thing to me. Oil companies need to work without worrying and international investors need to feel calm."[21] The fact that U.S. counter-narcotics aid had helped secure the oil operations of not only U.S. companies, but also Canadian firms, such as Calgary-based Petrobank Energy and Resources, was made evident by Cruz when he stated, "We are conducting better operations now because we have tools like helicopters, troops and training provided in large part by Plan Colombia."[22]

Despite more than $4 billion in U.S. funding, Plan Colombia never came close to achieving its principal counter-narcotics objective of reducing coca cultivation by 50 per cent in five years. In fact, according to statistics released by the U.S. Office of National Drug Control Policy (ONDCP), coca cultivation in Colombia was higher in 2005 than when Plan Colombia was initiated five years earlier. Furthermore, coca cultivation had spread from six of the country's thirty-two departments at the outset of Plan Colombia, to twenty-three by 2005.[23] Despite the failure of Plan Colombia to achieve its principal stated objective, the Bush administration extended it for another five years.

While Plan Colombia failed to achieve its counter-narcotics objectives, it did succeed in attaining the goals outlined by U.S. Energy Secretary Bill Richardson six years earlier: U.S. military aid would provide security for multinational energy companies. As a result, by 2005 the Colombian government's willingness to protect the operations of foreign energy companies, reduce the royalties these companies pay on the natural resources they extract and ensure they can freely repatriate their profits, made Colombia a poster child for neoliberalism.

Natural Resources and Human Rights

The increased exploitation of Colombia's natural resources for export under neoliberalism has devastated workers and communities in resource-rich regions. In fact, the statistics on human rights violations perpetrated in mining and oil regions of the country are staggering. For instance, an average of one union leader in the mining and energy sector is assassinated every month, and the military and its right-wing paramilitary allies are responsible for 97 per cent of the killings.[24] Between 1995 and 2002, 433 massacres occurred in mining municipalities, resulting—when combined with the number of people assassinated individually—in the killing of 6,626 peasants. Additionally, 68 per cent of Colombia's more than three million internally displaced persons—the second-largest internally displaced population in the world after the Sudan—were forcibly displaced from mining regions.[25]

In the neoliberal era, some of the world's largest multinational mining companies have become involved with the paramilitaries and human rights abuses in the regions in which they operate. The Alabama-based Drummond Company took advantage of the deregulation that was occurring under globalization by shifting its coal-producing operations overseas in the late 1980s, thereby dismantling the Fordist compact it was engaged in with U.S. mineworkers. Drummond purchased the open-pit Pribbenow Mine near the northern Colombian town of La Loma, as well as a Caribbean port for shipping its coal to the United States and other countries. In the ensuing years, the company boosted the Pribbenow Mine's coal production to more than twenty million tons annually, making it one of the largest coal mining operations in the world and the most significant contributor to Drummond's more than $1.5 billion annual revenues.[26]

Drummond's exploitation of cheaper Colombian coal, due in large part to the company paying low wages and receiving favourable concession terms from the Colombian government, allowed it to close five mines in Alabama and lay off seventeen hundred better-paid U.S. miners. The payroll savings for the company proved substantial, as Alabama mineworkers who earned US$18 an hour gave up their jobs to Colombian miners earning an hourly wage of US$2.45.[27] These payroll savings alone boosted Drummond's profits by more than a quarter of a million dollars annually—and that didn't include the additional savings from no longer having to provide expensive health insurance and other benefits to U.S. workers.

However, by choosing to do business in Colombia, Drummond became enmeshed in the country's civil conflict and the dirty war waged against unionists. In March 2001, a paramilitary death squad stopped a company bus carrying workers from the Pribbenow Mine, pulled two men off the bus and executed them. The victims, Valmore Locarno and Victor Hugo Orcasita, were the president and vice-president of the local chapter of the Colombian union Sintramienergetica, representing the mine's workers. Drummond had refused a request by the two union leaders, who were engaged in contract negotiations with the company at the time, to be allowed to sleep at the mine for fear of paramilitary threats. Seven months later, the union local's new president, Gustavo Soler Mora, was also taken from a company bus by paramilitaries and killed.

In 2002, a lawsuit was filed in U.S. federal court on behalf of Sintramienergetica claiming that the company had "aided and abetted" the paramilitary perpetrators of the murders. While Drummond denied the allegations, a sworn statement by former Colombian intelligence officer Rafael García supported the union's claims. In his statement, García said he witnessed Augusto Jiménez, president of Drummond's Colombia operations, hand over a "suitcase full of cash" to a paramilitary commander named Julian as payment for killing Locarno and Orcasita. Former paramilitary fighter Alberto Visbal verified García's statement, claiming that he was also present when Jiménez handed his commander $200,000 in cash.[28] The judge refused to allow the statements to be submitted as evidence, however, arguing that the case was beyond the discovery stage. Consequently, the jury found Drummond not guilty.

Another former paramilitary fighter claimed that Drummond had ongoing relations with the paramilitaries. In a sworn affidavit, he admitted collecting "taxes" from Drummond—20 to 32 cents per ton of coal—in return for his fighters providing protection for the company's coal trains.[29] It was not only Drummond's alleged ties to paramilitaries that enmeshed the company in the civil conflict, but also its relationship with the Colombian army. According to Captain Wilfredo González, commander of the two hundred Colombian soldiers stationed inside Drummond's Pribbenow Mine, the company provides fuel for the helicopters that his troops use to combat guerrillas who pose a threat to mining operations in the region.[30]

Drummond is not the only multinational company accused of maintaining ties to paramilitaries; the union representing Coca-Cola's workers in Colombia has claimed the soft drink manufacturer recruited paramilitaries to murder a labour leader at one of its Colombian bottling plants in 1996. Further links between multinational corporations and the right-wing death squads became evident in 2007, when Cincinnati-based Chiquita Brands pleaded guilty in a U.S. court to funding paramilitaries in the banana-growing region of northern Colombia. Between 1997 and 2004, Chiquita paid paramilitaries $1.7 million, even though the company knew that they were on the U.S. State Department's list of foreign terrorist organizations.[31]

In 2003, President Uribe began negotiations with the country's largest paramilitary organization, the United Self-Defence Forces of Colombia (Autodefesas Unidas de Colombia, AUC), with the goal of demobilizing its fighters. The two parties agreed that, in return for demobilizing their troops and confessing their crimes, paramilitary leaders would serve no more than eight years in prison. By March 2006, more than thirty thousand paramilitaries had demobilized and were receiving monthly payments from the government under the Justice and Peace law, which established the legal process for the demobilization.

Despite the official face of the demobilization, human rights organizations claimed that many paramilitaries did not actually lay down their weapons and that the process represented more of a restructuring than an actual disbandment of AUC. Amnesty International reported in late 2005 that paramilitaries in Medellín were still active in the city's poor barrios almost two years after they had supposedly demobilized.[32] In 2006, the Colombian NGO Indepaz revealed that 43 new paramilitary groups with a total of 4,000 fighters had formed in 22 of the country's 32 departments.[33] Human rights lawyer Alirio Uribe echoed these claims:

> There are forty-three new paramilitary groups but, according to the Ministry of Defence, these new paramilitary groups have nothing to do with the old ones. But the truth is, they are the

same. Before they were the AUC, now they are called the New Generation AUC. They have the same collusion with the army and the police. It's a farce.[34]

According to a report issued by the Colombian Commission of Jurists, paramilitaries were responsible for a majority of the killings of civilians during President Uribe's first term in office (2002-2006), despite the fact that they were supposedly engaged in a ceasefire during demobilization talks. In fact, the Colombian military and the paramilitaries together accounted for 75 percent of the killings of civilians during that four-year period with the guerrillas being responsible for the remaining 25 percent.[35]

Sintramienergetica union officials and local residents claim that paramilitaries continue to operate in the vicinity of Drummond's Pribbenow Mine, despite being supposedly demobilized. As one resident, who requested anonymity for security reasons, stated, "The demobilization of the paramilitaries here hasn't achieved anything. Everything's still the same."[36] In June 2006, the continuation of paramilitary activity directly affected Sintramienergetica when Alvaro Mercado, a member of the union's executive committee, survived an assassination attempt made against him by two gunmen outside his home. In reference to the relationship between Drummond's private security force, the Colombian army and the paramilitaries, Mercado stated, "The security guards, the army and the paramilitaries are all the same. They all work with the company. Drummond provides vehicles and gasoline to the paramilitaries inside the company's installations, including the Pribbenow Mine."[37]

The constantly expanding open-pit coal mine is also proving harmful to the local environment, despite claims by Drummond that its operations are environmentally sound. At the entrance to the Pribbenow Mine is a large billboard that boldly declares, "We are committed to the preservation of the environment." Another billboard displays beautiful colour photos of wild animals and a declaration prohibiting the killing of those creatures on company property. But it is difficult to ignore the contradiction. The operator of one of the world's largest open-pit coal mines portrays itself as environmentally friendly and a protector of animals, at the same time its ever-expanding operations are devouring every tree and plant that constitute the natural habitat of the local wildlife.

As the Pribbenow Mine has grown, Drummond has contributed to infrastructure improvements in the nearby town of La Loma, including paving the main street. However, the fact that it is the only paved road in town is not always evident, due to the abundance of sand-coloured dust that covers its entire length. The dust, generated by the company's giant 25,000-acre open-pit mine permeates everything in La Loma: roads, vehicles, homes, clothes and people. According to one local resident, "Many people here suffer from respiratory ailments due to the dust in the air."[38] Drummond's website proudly states that the Pribbenow Mine has a positive impact on the local economy and that the company "contributes to social programs to improve the lives of its employees and neighbours by providing assistance to schools, hospitals, and churches in the communities around its existing operations."[39] But several local residents claim that the company's social programs do not begin to offset the negative social and health consequences caused by its mining operations. Meanwhile, Drummond, like many other foreign mining companies, has earned record profits from its operations in rural Colombia, where 85 per cent of the population continues to live in poverty.

Canada and Colombian Coal

The Canadian government has played a significant role in establishing favourable investment conditions in Colombia for multinational mining companies. In 2001, the country's mining code was rewritten by the Canadian International Development Agency (CIDA), the Calgary-based industry think tank Canadian Energy Research Institute (CERI), Colombia's Ministry of Mines and the Colombian law firm Martínez, Córdoba and Associates—at the time representing half of the mining companies registered in Colombia. Undoubtedly, part of Ottawa's motive for participating in such an industry-biased process was the fact that many Canadian mining companies were operating in Colombia, including Greystar Resources, BMR Gold, Conquistador Mines, Colombia Goldfields and Coalcorp, which operates in the same region as Drummond's Pribbenow Mine.

The new CIDA-backed code relaxed environmental regulations on mining operations, extended the length of concessions issued to foreign corporations and, perhaps most importantly, reduced the royalty rates that companies are required to pay to the Colombian government. Article 227 of the new code reduces the royalty rates on coal from 10-15 per cent to a mere 0.4 per cent.[40] In reference to the new royalty rates, Francisco Ramírez, president of the Colombian State Mineworkers' Union (Sintraminercol), declared, "With the stroke of a pen, once again the Nation lost enormous sums of money which could have been used to address social problems, like the fact that 80 children in Colombia perish every day from hunger, malnutrition, and curable diseases."[41]

CIDA justified its role in the development of the new mining code by declaring, "Canadian energy and mining sector companies with an interest in Colombia will benefit from the development of a stable, consistent and familiar operating environment in this resource-rich developing economy."[42] Ramírez, who has survived seven assassination attempts made against him by paramilitaries because of his outspoken criticism of neoliberalism, labelled CIDA's role as "Canadian manipulation to benefit foreign companies to the detriment of Colombians." He went on to note, "The new code flexibilised environmental regulations, diminished labour guarantees for workers and opened the property of Afro-Colombian and indigenous people to exploitation."[43]

The new mining code appears to ensure a continuation, if not an intensification, of the forced displacement of rural communities in Colombia. In the neoliberal era, millions of Colombian peasants have been displaced from lands that contain resources sought by multinational corporations. While political refugees have gained increased international attention over the years, the plight of these economic refugees has largely gone unnoticed. As authors such as Peter Newell have noted, the number of troubled relationships between corporations and communities has increased in recent years as neoliberalism has systematically lowered barriers to trade. Newell argues that it is poorer communities in particular that are placed at risk under globalization.[44] While we should rightfully identify these communities as stakeholders in the process of economic development, in Colombia's civil conflict they often become "subversives," seen as standing in the way of corporate access to valuable resources. Right-wing paramilitaries and private security companies then often target those individuals who dare to defend the rights of communities.

One community deemed to be standing in the way of corporate access to valuable resources was the small Afro-Colombian town of Tabaco, located in the semi-arid department of La Guajira on Colombia's Caribbean coast. In this case, the multinational owners of the Cerrejón mine wanted to expand their open-pit coal operation to increase exports to eastern Canada, the United States and Europe. The mine, along with a private railroad and port, was constructed in the 1980s, with the help of a $160 million loan from Canada's Export Development Bank.[45] At the time, the mine was jointly owned by U.S.-based Exxon—which merged with Mobil in 1999 to become ExxonMobil—and the state-owned company Carbones de Colombia S.A. (Carbocol). The mine, however, provided no economic benefits to those Colombians living in the communities on its periphery. The jobs went to outsiders transported to and from the mining complex in company buses.

By the late 1990s, the Cerrejón mine had become the world's largest open-pit coal mine, a massive hole in the ground, measuring 45 kilometres long and 8 kilometres across. In 2000, to comply with neoliberal reforms demanded by the IMF, the Colombian government privatized Carbocol, selling its 50 per cent share in the Cerrejón mine to a consortium of multinational mining companies—Anglo American (British), BHP Billiton (Australian) and Glencore (Swiss). In 2002, ExxonMobil sold its 50 per cent share in the mine to the consortium, which became the sole owner. Then, four years later, Glencore sold its one-third share in the consortium to another Swiss multinational mining company, Xstrata.

Over the years, the workers at the Cerrejón mine have had to endure repressive tactics employed by the State on behalf of the company—not unlike the repression suffered by Cape Breton's mineworkers almost a century earlier. In early 1990, for example, negotiations between the mine's owners and the union over pay and working conditions broke down. The miners responded by engaging initially in a work slowdown and then, on April 25, by going out on strike. Eighteen days into the work stoppage, according to historian Aviva Chomsky:

> Colombian President Virgilio Barco invoked an obscure provision of Colombia's Constitution and asked the Supreme Court to empower him to declare the strike illegal because it was "potentially damaging" to the country's economy. [...] He then au-

thorized the Colombian Army to occupy the mine. In May 1990, eight hundred armed soldiers in armoured tanks forced the workers to return to work.[46]

The Colombian army would again be deployed during future negotiations to defend the interests of the mine's owners. Then, in 2004, union negotiators engaged in talks with the company received death threats from paramilitaries.[47]

Communities located on the periphery of the giant mine have also endured repression and human rights abuses at the hands of the Cerrejón Mine Company. In 1997, the mine's owners convinced the Colombian government to displace the Afro-Colombian farming community of Tabaco, whose residents were descendents of escaped slaves and had subsisted for generations on farming. Realizing that their displacement was inevitable, the residents of the town requested that the company negotiate with them to collectively relocate the community so they could preserve their livelihoods and social networks. In 1998, community members formed the Committee to Relocate Tabaco and demanded that the Cerrejón Mine Company negotiate collectively with them. The company refused, insisting instead on negotiating with individual property owners.

Many residents settled with the company out of fear that they would not receive anything if they continued to demand a collective relocation. Some 700 residents, however, continued to resist and, on August 9, 2001, were forcibly evicted from their homes by two hundred of the State's security forces and the mine's private guards. The entire town was then bulldozed and incorporated into the mine. According to one resident, Emilio Ramón Pérez:

> The police beat and broke my head in four places and took me out of the house. I was unconscious in the hospital for twenty days. They destroyed my house without letting me take my things. They took everything: my refrigerator, stove, television, chairs, they took all of my things.[48]

Many of Tabaco's homeless families became economic refugees, joining the ranks of Colombia's three million internally displaced persons. Some of them fled the region for a life of hardship in Colombia's cities, while others moved to neighbouring communities, determined to continue their fight for a collective relocation. In May 2002, they successfully petitioned Colombia's Supreme Court, which ruled that the municipality of Hatonuevo, in which Tabaco was located, must allocate resources to build new homes for the displaced residents. But such resources were scarce, and the villagers of Tabaco had no means of ensuring that the court's ruling would be implemented. The new homes were not built, and José Julio Pérez, president of the Committee to Relocate Tabaco, explained that they have had little success in their struggle because "the mining company has undue influence over local government officials as well as the army and police due to the country's endemic corruption."[49]

Tabaco is not the only Afro-Colombian community that has been threatened by the Cerrejón Mine. Several others are facing displacement, including the community of Chancleta. By 2002, most of Chancleta's residents had already been forced to abandon their homes, due to their inability to support themselves. They had lost that ability when the mine purchased much of the unoccupied land surrounding the remote village and then denied residents access to it. As a result, villagers could no longer hunt and fish, and their goats had nowhere to graze. The mine was, effectively, starving the villagers out. The partial abandonment of Chancleta suggests that the multinational owners of the mine had devised a strategy to force villagers to "voluntarily" vacate their properties, thereby allowing the company to avoid replicating the conflict that had resulted from Tabaco's displacement.

To address some of the social and economic problems related to the mine and the 185-kilometre railway line used to transport the coal to the company's private port on the Caribbean coast, the mine's owners established the Cerrejón Foundation in 1984. According to executive director Yolanda Mendoza, the Foundation provides micro-credit programs for small businesses and local communities, along with field staff to teach these communities new farming techniques. However, it has implemented none of the projects in the immediate vicinity of the mine, where communities are destined for future displacement. When asked what the Foundation was doing to help communities displaced by the mine, Mendoza replied, "They are not really displaced. They are not displaced because there are no communities where the mine is at this time. There was a process a long time ago, but now there are no communities there." When reminded of the recent destruction of Tabaco, Mendoza became visibly tense and stated, "I don't think that is true. But it is a topic you have to speak about with the Cerrejón Mine Company, because I don't have the authority to talk about it."[50]

When asked about the issue, a spokesperson for the mine, Ricardo Plata Cepeda, said the company was waiting for the Colombian courts to determine how much it had to pay those forcibly displaced from Tabaco.[51] Undoubtedly, the mine's owners knew full well that there would be little likelihood of judicial rulings being effectively enforced—as already evidenced by the municipal government's failure to abide by the Supreme Court's ruling. Meanwhile, the Colombian government extended the company's operating contract until 2034, and by that time, given the mine's current rate of growth, the dominant feature in the landscape of southern La Guajira will be an ecologically devastating 100-by-18 kilometre hole in the ground.

In October 2004, the leader of Colombia's state mineworkers' union, Francisco Ramírez, went into temporary exile in the United States, following the seventh assassination attempt made against him in fourteen years. Two months later, he visited Cape Breton to help raise awareness about the human rights issues linked to the importation of Colombian coal by Nova Scotia Power (NSP).[52] NSP refused to meet with Ramírez because, as a company spokesperson stated, "Nova Scotia Power does not become involved in human rights issues in the countries from which it purchases coal. The company is only concerned with two things: price and quality."[53] Ramírez did, however, meet with Bob Burchell, the local representative of the United Mineworkers of America. Afterward, the Canadian union leader discussed the human rights crisis in Colombia, saying that, "Nova Scotia, unfortunately, is contributing to that. Every time we flip that light, we are contributing to what is going on in Colombia. Not because we want to but because we have no choice because we're controlled by a monopoly of power right now in Nova Scotia. We should not be relying on blood-soaked coal from Colombia to turn our lights on when we have ample supplies of coal here."[54]

NSP again refused to meet with Ramírez on the Colombian unionist's subsequent visit to Nova Scotia in March 2005. But, in response to a growing public campaign and increased media coverage of the issue, the utility company agreed to meet with Tabaco community leader José Julio Pérez in March 2006. NSP representatives met with Pérez in a luxurious boardroom—by rural Colombian standards—on the sixteenth floor of the company's headquarters in Halifax, Nova Scotia. One NSP representative stared across the large table at Pérez—an impoverished Colombian peasant who, along with his wife and four children, had been homeless for the previous five years, after being forcibly displaced by the Cerrejón mine—and had the audacity to open the meeting by callously stating that the company's principal concern was its public image.[55] The NSP representatives then listened to Pérez state his case, but the company ultimately refused to use its leverage as a customer to publicly pressure the Cerrejón mine into negotiating a collective relocation of the displaced residents of Tabaco. Thereafter, NSP would refer Nova Scotians to the website of the Cerrejón Mine Company so they could learn about the social projects that the mine was implementing in local communities.

As previously mentioned, however, there were no social projects being implemented—neither by the Cerrejón Mine Company nor the Colombian State—in the communities most directly affected by mining operations. In fact, according to historian Aviva Chomsky, the Colombian army is the country's principal representative in the mining region in La Guajira. As Chomsky notes, "Practically the only state presence in Guajira where the Cerrejón mine is located is the army. Schools, roads, healthcare and other social services are almost non-existent. Paramilitaries operate freely and profits flow out freely. It's a neoliberal paradise."[56]

This repressive context ensured that the community of Tabaco did not come to the table as an equal player in a stakeholder process. After years of harassment from the Cerrejón Mine Company, Tabaco residents were pressured by the mine's owners to engage in a process of individual negotiations and were offered money in exchange for their houses and land. The nature of this "negotiation" process reflects the complex political aspects of corporate-community relationships where differing cultural perceptions of ownership and rights, not to mention communication, become evident.

Critics of corporate capitalism have long pointed to the need to integrate indigenous and alternative cultural perspectives into stakeholder discussions around community development initiatives. These calls are reflected in international agreements such as the International Labour Organization's Convention 169, which requires corporations and governments to actively engage indigenous communities in dialogue on all issues affecting "the persons, institutions, property, labour, cultures and environment of the peoples concerned."[57] In the case of Tabaco, community members demanded that the mine negotiate with the town as a whole so that their integrity as a cultural and economic community could be safeguarded. The Cerrejón mine Company, however, insisted on a negotiation process based on the capitalist concept of individual ownership rights.

In 2007, in response to an investigation launched by the Organization for Economic Co-operation and Development (OECD)— as well as pressure from the mine's workers and from public campaigns waged in Canada, the United States, Australia and Europe on behalf of the displaced villagers of Tabaco—the Cerrejón Mine Company agreed to negotiate collectively with communities to be displaced in the future. Eventually, in 2008, the mine's owners agreed to negotiate a collective relocation of the displaced residents of Tabaco.

The capitalist development model that has made Colombian coal available for multinationals to exploit and export to the wealthy nations of the global North is indicative of what is occurring throughout the South under neoliberalism. Indian physicist and philosopher Vandana Shiva has criticized this development model, as well as the accepted wisdom behind it. Shiva dismisses the widely held belief that people suffer from poverty in the South simply because they have yet to achieve the same level of capitalist industrialization as the North. She says that it is essential to understand the true causes of poverty:

> The poor are not those who have been "left behind"; they are the ones who have been robbed. The riches accumulated by Europe are based on riches taken from Asia, Africa and Latin America. Without the destruction of India's rich textile industry, without the takeover of the spice trade, without the genocide of the native American tribes, without Africa's slavery, the Industrial Revolution would not have led to new riches for Europe or the U.S. It was this violent takeover of Third World resources and markets that created wealth in the North and poverty in the South.[58]

Suzanne MacNeil, in her article "Reflections on Mining in Colombia: When 'Development' Creates Deprivation," suggests that the plight of the communities affected by the operations of the Cerrejón Mine Company is a clear illustration of Shiva's argument.

MacNeil describes how Colombia's IMF-pushed development model destroyed a sustainable community in La Guajira, thereby creating, rather than alleviating, poverty. Emilio Pérez, a displaced resident of Tabaco, corroborates MacNeil's contention: "Life was rich, we shared, and no one suffered because we shared what we had. There was a river near the town. We had land. We walked freely all over the territory. But the last nine years we have had no land to work. We are displaced, and we have no home."[59]

MacNeil claims that the Cerrejón mine epitomizes the model of so-called development that the IMF and the World Bank are imposing on countries of the global South. However, despite claims by these institutions that neoliberalism would alleviate the poverty that plagues so many in the South, MacNeil suggests that, in reality:

> Their "solutions" have led to an exacerbation of poverty, which is not entirely surprising since their prescriptions are aimed at increasing economic indicators that more closely follow the profit levels of corporations than the actual well-being of people. Herein lies the fatal flaw of this model: increasing the profits of foreign investors depends on weakening the governmental regulations that protect people from the predatory actions that disrupt well-established communities and cultures of self-sustainability. [...] As the plight of the communities in the Guajira illustrates, it is unacceptable to pursue the outright destruction of sustainable cultures in favour of benefiting an ecologically moribund industry that creates jobs in the short term. At its most fundamental level, economic development policy should first do no harm. And, as Shiva points out in reference to the North's "charitable" efforts to alleviate poverty in the South, "It's not about how much more we can give, so much as how much less we can take."[60]

Yet capitalist elites in the global North continue to impose a development model on countries such as Colombia that allow the North to keep "taking." Colombia's experiences in the extractive sectors under neoliberalism make evident the intricate web of connections between the global North and South in an unfolding story of poverty, displacement, human rights violations and expatriation of profits. We argue that these are not exceptions in the "inevitable" process of neoliberal globalization, as capitalist elites would have us believe. Rather, these features are entirely functional to the model.

The Human Cost of Free Trade

The dismantling of the Keynesian-inspired ISI model and the implementation of neoliberalism has made Colombia's natural resources available for increased exploitation by multinational corporations. As a result, oil and coal have surpassed coffee to become the country's two leading legal exports. President Uribe's neoliberal reforms have resulted in Colombia achieving impressive levels of economic growth, although the majority of Colombians have not benefited from it. At the same time, U.S.-backed security policies have safeguarded the operations of multinational corporations in Colombia by targeting not only leftist guerrillas but also non-violent sectors of civil society that are critical of neoliberalism. Ultimately, the social consequences of globalization have proven devastating for a majority of Colombians, as evidenced by the continued high levels of poverty and inequality, the expansion of the informal economy, and killings and forced displacement under the dirty war waged by capitalist elites.

Nowhere is the brutality of the dirty war and State-sanctioned displacement more evident than in Colombia's mining regions. Afro-Colombian and indigenous communities are being forcibly displaced in La Guajira to allow for the exploitation and exportation of Colombian coal so that people in the global North can maintain their relatively comfortable lifestyles. In addition to the repressive actions of the Cerrejón Mine Company and the Colombian State, the dirty war has also reared its ugly head in La Guajira. In April 2004, in the village of Bahía Portete, which is situated adjacent to the Cerrejón mine's private port, right-wing paramilitaries massacred twelve indigenous Wayuu. Another thirty members of the community were "disappeared" and more than three hundred forcibly displaced. One villager, Debora Barros Fince, described the attack on the community, which was eerily reminiscent of the provincial police's rampage through the streets of the Whitney Pier neighbourhood of Sydney, Cape Breton, more than eighty years earlier:

> About one hundred and fifty soldiers entered the village on the morning of the 18th; they were from the army so people didn't react. But then the soldiers started attacking people. They broke my grandmother's legs. They tied one boy to the back of a Toyota

truck and dragged him along the street. When people realized what was happening they tried to run away. Most of them escaped. But the soldiers caught some of them and turned them over to men in civilian clothes. Those men were the paramilitaries who had arrived in the community a few months earlier. It was the paramilitaries who did the killing.[61]

Some locals have speculated that the massacre was part of a paramilitary strategy to consolidate control over drug trafficking routes, while others have suggested it was motivated by land speculation, due to rumours that the Cerrejón mine intended to expand its port in the coming years. Whatever the reason, the massacre appears to be related to the increased international trade occurring under neoliberal globalization. The increased trade between Colombia and Cape Breton has made it easier for drug traffickers to export Colombia's most famous product—cocaine—to North America. In June 2004, only two months after the massacre, 83 kilograms of cocaine were discovered on a ship transporting coal to Sydney, Cape Breton.[62] The ship belonged to Canada Steamship Lines, a company owned by the sons of Paul Martin, Canada's prime minister at the time.

Three

The New Economy in Cape Breton and Atlantic Canada

Since 1999, ships laden with Colombian coal for delivery to Nova Scotia Power (NSP) have regularly arrived in Sydney harbour and other Nova Scotia ports. With NSP's shift to Colombian coal and the related closing of Cape Breton's mines, Nova Scotia has become a significant importer of coal. This shift is part of a broader trend under neoliberal globalization in which companies throughout the global North have increasingly turned to the global South for cheaper resources and labour. At the same time, Cape Bretoners, and Canadians in general, have been inundated with political rhetoric and media reports suggesting that the loss of decent paying manufacturing jobs is an inescapable reality of the new global economy. Furthermore, pro-free traders often portray neoliberal globalization as an inevitable "evolutionary" process, rather than what it really is: an ideologically motivated economic model implemented through conscious policy decisions. And then, by logical extension, they tell people that they must learn to adapt to this "inevitable" new economic reality in order to remain competitive.

One way in which Cape Bretoners have "adapted" to the new economy is by abandoning the island for jobs elsewhere. While coal imports have increased over the past decade, Cape Breton's leading export has been its people. Industrial Cape Breton, or Cape Breton Regional Municipality (CBRM), saw its population decline by more than 10 per cent between 1996 and 2006, from 117,849 to 105,928.[1] While Cape Bretoners have, historically, left the island in search of work during economic downturns, they have never before emigrated in such large numbers over such a short time. A 2004 Labour Market Review published by Service Canada pointed to neoliberal globalization—without actually using the term—as being responsible for the loss of jobs and the shifting nature of employment in Cape Breton: "At least some of the declines are because of gradual downsizing and shutdowns experienced in the coal mining and steel manufacturing industries. These structural changes in Cape Breton's industrial base as well as the global emergence of service industries are partly responsible for recent changes in the composition of employment on the Island."[2]

One change in the composition of employment in Cape Breton under neoliberalism has been the shift in the gender makeup of the workforce. With the decline in industrial jobs and an increase in service sector employment, the percentage of jobs held by men declined from 59 per cent in 1987 to 48 per cent in 2005.[3] The fact that a greater percentage of women than men now work in Cape Breton is also reflected in a gender breakdown of unemployment rates, as 18 per cent of men were unemployed in 2005, compared with only 11 per cent of women.[4]

Many unemployed Cape Breton men, along with thousands of other Atlantic Canadians, have moved to Alberta to work in the oil sands. In 2006 alone, more than 13,000 Atlantic Canadians made the move out west. It is estimated that another 12,000 Atlantic Canadians "commute" to and from the oil-rich province. These "six and two'ers" fly out to the oil sands for six weeks of work and then back home for two weeks off before returning for another six weeks on the job.[5] In many cases, these migrant Cape Bretoners and commuters send money back home to help struggling relatives. By exporting its people and becoming partially dependent on remittances, Cape Breton in the neoliberal era has come to reflect some of the social and economic realities of Colombia and other countries in the global South. However, a remittance-based economy is not a viable development model if one wishes to preserve close-knit family and community ties as well as cultural practices.

The Call Centre Phenomenon

The laying off of Cape Breton coal miners and steelworkers throughout the 1990s and the eventual shutting down of those industries in

2001 dramatically increased unemployment rates. But the increase was only temporary, as a combination of out-migration and the creation of new jobs soon reduced the number of unemployed in Cape Breton to 15.5 per cent in 2004, down from 23.7 per cent a decade earlier.[6] Proponents of neoliberalism praise business-friendly policies for creating a dramatic increase in the number of service sector jobs, not only in Cape Breton but also throughout Canada, as well as corresponding low levels of unemployment in many parts of the country. While big-box stores and chain restaurants account for many service sector jobs, it is the "call centre" that has come to epitomize the industry. By 2000, there were an estimated 13,400 call centres in Canada, employing a workforce of more than half a million people.[7]

Globalization has made it easy for multinational corporations to move their operations from one country to another, taking advantage of the most favourable economic conditions available. However, many U.S. companies are restricted by language when deciding where to establish their customer service operations. Consequently, to locate the cheapest English-speaking workforce they often seek out the most economically depressed areas in North America. Cities and towns experiencing industrial decline fit the bill perfectly. Their relatively educated workforces and high unemployment rates ensure a surplus of cheap skilled workers to fill service sector jobs that pay below average wages, provide few benefits and offer little job security. In some ways, the new service sector economy represents the global North's version of the informal economy that has emerged under neoliberalism in Colombia and other nations of the global South.

Neoliberalism in Canada has also intensified competition between provinces to attract investment and jobs. Basically, this competition amounts to a race to the bottom, similar to what is occurring between nations of the global South. It is a race in which Canada's municipal and provincial governments desperately offer corporations the cheapest and most flexible labour, generous subsidies, and low tax rates to attract jobs and generate economic growth. In Cape Breton, as in other parts of Canada, establishing favourable economic conditions for call centres has been promoted as the solution to hardships brought on by de-industrialization. Indeed, pro-neoliberal politicians have worked hard to create a business-friendly environment throughout Canada. Many of them even brag about their achievements, as evidenced in a column penned by Nova Scotia's Conservative premier Rodney MacDonald in March 2006. MacDonald's column was published in the *Chronicle Herald* following the release of a study conducted by accounting giant KPMG, which ranked the best places for companies to do business. The study compared 128 cities in nine industrialized nations in North America, Europe and Asia with regard to the costs incurred by businesses in such areas as labour, facilities, transportation, utilities and taxes. The study ranked the Cape Breton city of Sydney among the top ten most business-friendly places in Canada and in the top twelve among countries surveyed. In all, four Nova Scotia cities—Sydney, Halifax, Truro and Pictou—ranked in the top ten business-friendly places in Canada.[8]

In his column, MacDonald revelled in the high rankings achieved by cities in the province and asked, "What sets Nova Scotia apart from the rest?" He went on to explain: "Over the last six years our government has worked hard to make Nova Scotia a business-friendly environment—and we're seeing positive results." MacDonald then described some of the province's business-friendly policies by explaining how his government is "finally getting rid of the Business Occupancy Assessment Tax" and that Nova Scotia's "Industrial Expansion Fund is helping the economy by providing assistance in the form of loan guarantees." He concluded his piece by proudly declaring, "Nova Scotia is a great place to do business, indeed."[9]

MacDonald openly bragged about reducing business taxes and increasing corporate subsidies to make Nova Scotia one of the most business-friendly places in the world. However, he conspicuously omitted other factors, such as low labour costs, that have also contributed to the province achieving such "positive results." With his rousing endorsement of KPMG's findings, MacDonald was basically telling Nova Scotians that they should be proud of the fact that they are willing—or are forced—to work for lower wages than most other workers in the industrialized world; that they should be happy corporate tax cuts either shift a greater share of the tax burden onto individuals or result in cutbacks to public programs; and that Nova Scotians should be thankful their tax dollars are subsidizing foreign companies while the health care system deteriorates and post-secondary students pay the highest tuition in the country.

It is the establishment of such business-friendly policies under neoliberalism that has led to the economy of Cape Breton and other de-industrialized communities becoming dependent on call centres, many of which are those of U.S. companies. The policies of governments like Rodney MacDonald's illustrate the hypocrisy of neoliberalism: while neoliberals call for repeated cutbacks in government spending, the subsidy spigot remains open for corporations.

The establishment of a business-friendly environment is driven by the desire to achieve economic growth and create jobs. Elected officials often see attracting multinational corporations as a quick fix in their attempts to attain these objectives. As political scientist James Bickerton and community economic development expert Theresa MacNeil point out:

> The multinational corporation ... is the most sought after external investor, comprising from the policy-maker's point of view the development equivalent of a "turn-key" operation. Of course, this kind of "total package" option has its downside. Because the large multinational corporation acts as a self-contained and footloose agent, it has significant leverage in the global marketplace, forcing regions seeking to play host to such operations to compete with each other for the privilege. Moreover, even if successful in this competitive bidding, regions immediately become vulnerable to subsequent corporate decisions to disinvest. And the "development footprint" of such self-contained operations can be quite small, in the sense that local resources, suppliers and networks are often left undeveloped, quite simply because the large corporation does not need them. Investment of this sort, then, while welcomed for the jobs it creates, usually fails to increase the overall flexibility and capacity of the local economy.[10]

The provincial governments in Nova Scotia and New Brunswick have followed the development path described by Bickerton and MacNeil, competing with each other to offer the most appealing packages of subsidies and other financial incentives to multinational companies seeking the most cost-effective locations to establish their customer service operations. In New Brunswick, between 1991 and 2000, the provincial government provided call centres, including one owned by UPS (United Parcel Service), with $50 million in "forgivable" loans and grants to entice them to set up shop in the province. The forgivable loans did not have to be repaid to

New Brunswick taxpayers if the companies met specified employment targets, thereby turning the loans into subsidies. The provincial government also provided funding to cover 10 per cent of a call centre's payroll for its first three years of operation. The provincial government went even further, providing funding to cover the costs of training call centre workers and eliminating the 11 per cent provincial sales tax on call centre telephone numbers.[11] Consequently, at the same time that the government was cutting funding for social services, it was providing substantial subsidies for multinational corporations in return for low-paying jobs that often proved only temporary. Furthermore, increases in university tuition costs as a result of cuts in education funding resulted in more students having to work throughout the year, thereby providing another source of cheap labour for call centres and other service sector companies in the new economy.

The temporary nature of call centre jobs and the overall difficulties involved in organizing workers in the service sector has helped preserve the low wages of the call centre industry. In fact, the New Brunswick government has proudly promoted the province's anti-union stance on the website of its Department of Economic Development and Tourism. To entice call centre investment, the government declared: "New Brunswick has the lowest rate of unionization in Canada ... NBTel is the only telephone company in Canada with non-unionized clerical employees.... There has never been an industry attempt to unionize [call centres in the province]."[12] These business-friendly practices have succeeded in generating both employment and economic growth in New Brunswick. Since the early 1990s, the province has attracted more than fourteen thousand call centre jobs, which has lowered unemployment.

New Brunswick's neoliberal policies have forced neighbouring provinces to offer similar incentives to corporations in order to compete. In 2001, for example, the Nova Scotia government paid $7.5 million to U.S.-based Xerox in return for the company creating six hundred call centre jobs in Halifax. Xerox pointed to the city's business-friendly environment as a factor in its decision when it declared that "Halifax's educated workforce, advanced telecommunications infrastructure and friendly investment climate make it a perfect location."[13] Nova Scotia's minister of economic development, Gordon

Balser, echoed the company's sentiments by declaring that Xerox's decision to set up shop in Halifax "is signaling that our province is the right place to achieve its business objectives."[14]

During the ensuing years, Nova Scotia's government provided generous subsidies to many more call centre companies willing to establish operations in the province. In 2003, U.S.-based TeleTech received $11.8 million from the province to set up call centre operations in Halifax and Amherst.[15] Another American company, Convergys, was subsidized to the tune of $3.2 million in 2005 and the following year U.S.-based Citco Group received $7 million of Nova Scotia taxpayers' money.[16] In April 2007, the provincial government agreed to provide almost $1 million to U.S.-based Servicom for the expansion of its Sydney operation, which provided customer service for several U.S. companies including General Motors, AT&T, Allstate and ComCast.[17] Then, in October 2007, Premier Rodney MacDonald announced that Paragon Advanced Development, a call centre company from Bermuda, operating in Canada under the name Ignition, would expand its Halifax operations and create up to 150 new jobs over the next five years. Among the incentives provided to Paragon by the province was $1.2 million of taxpayers' money to help cover the company's payroll expenses and $300,000 for recruiting and training new employees.[18]

Not surprisingly, call centres quickly established themselves as the most prominent feature of the new economy in post-industrial Cape Breton. In March 2000, Prime Minister Jean Chrétien arrived in Sydney on the same day that the provincial government announced it was shutting down the city's steel plant. The prime minister and local politicians spoke about the good times that lay ahead for Cape Bretoners in the post-industrial age, and Chrétien, speaking in reference to the emergence of the call centre industry, announced that Sydney was becoming "a leader in the global knowledge-based economy."[19] Other elected officials espoused platitudes about how creatively Cape Breton was adapting to the new economy. The fact that the new "knowledge-based" jobs paid significantly less than the old industrial ones was conveniently omitted from the rhetoric. As political scientist Thom Workman explains:

> It is unlikely that we will ever hear a local politician say: "We endorse policies aimed at rolling your families out of $20-per-hour jobs and into $9-per-hour jobs. That is our goal. You older folks

Gibbs and Leech

may have enjoyed respectable, high-paying jobs with decent benefits and long-term security in the past, but we would like to see your children working in non-unionized, low-paying jobs."[20]

Under the new economy, the employment picture in post-industrial Sydney has shifted dramatically as higher paying, unionized industrial jobs have been replaced with lower paying, non-union work in the service sector. Between 1998 and 2002, six call centres were established in Cape Breton Regional Municipality. The call centres employed 3,650 people in 2002 with a payroll of $49.2 million. Many positions paid a starting wage of $9 per hour and, according to a 2003 study conducted by the consulting firm Canmac Economics, the majority of call centre workers earned an annual salary of between $15,000 and $20,000.[21] Meanwhile, Canada's poverty line—officially known as the Low Income Cut-Off (LICO)—for an individual was $16,160 at the time that the call centres were established.[22]

Richard MacNeil, a 49-year-old former steelworker who worked at an EDS call centre in Sydney, saw his pay drop from the $16 an hour he earned in the steel plant to $8.75 in his new job. MacNeil said the call centre work was stressful and the bosses at EDS "expected dedication and devotion for little more than minimum wage."[23] Luckily, the former steelworker was not solely reliant on his call centre paycheque, because he was also receiving a small pension from his former job in the steel plant. But MacNeil claimed that many of his fellow workers were dependent on their call centre income and, as a result, were struggling to survive. According to the former steelworker, "I'd talk to one woman in the smoke room at EDS and one day she was crying because it was such a struggle for her to be able to pay rent and bills every month. She barely had money left for food. She'd have been better off on welfare."[24]

And while Cape Bretoners were being offered jobs that paid poverty-level wages, U.S. call centre companies EDS, Stream and Upsource received more than $24 million in federal subsidies in 2000 and 2001, in addition to financial incentives provided by the province and municipality.[25] In effect, the federal and provincial governments were subsidizing U.S. companies that offered low-paying, non-unionized service sector jobs just as they had subsidized U.S. financier Henry Melville Whitney a century earlier for providing low-paid, non-unionized industrial sector jobs in the steel plant.

A look at the city of Sault Ste. Marie in Ontario illustrates how de-industrialization and the shift to the new service sector economy are not unique to Sydney or other Maritimes localities. The economic history of Sault Ste. Marie, a working-class city of 74,000, has paralleled that of Sydney in many ways over the past hundred years. Its industrialization process occurred in the early 20th century and revolved around steel production. Like Sydney, its industrial decline also occurred under neoliberal globalization. The workforce at Sault Ste. Marie's Algoma steel plant was reduced from 12,000 in the 1980s to 3,000 in 2002, due to the company's inability to compete with cheap imports in the new global economy.[26] The socio-economic impact on Sault Ste. Marie was similar to that which occurred in Cape Breton, as the city's unemployment rate rose to almost 20 per cent in the mid-1990s. But, by 2004, Sault Ste. Marie's jobless rate had dropped to only 9 per cent, due to the same two phenomena affecting Cape Breton: out-migration and the development of a service sector economy.

Four call centre companies—three of them American—established themselves in Sault Ste. Marie during the 1990s and were, by the end of 2004, employing 3,000 people. But the wages the call centre workers earned were markedly lower than those of the steelworkers. In 2004, the average call centre worker was non-unionized and earned $10 per hour with few or no benefits. The total payroll for the 3,000 workers employed by the four call centres amounted to $60 million. Meanwhile, in the same year, the steel plant paid an equivalent number of steelworkers $250 million in wages and benefits—more than four times as much as the call centres.[27] Clearly, the standard of living for many workers, and by extension many families, in Sault Ste. Marie had declined dramatically since the onset of de-industrialization.

A clear illustration of the insecurity of the service industry and its lack of commitment to local communities was Dell Computer's closing of its call centre in Edmonton, Alberta, in 2008. The call centre had only been in operation for three years when the company laid off its 900 workers as a result of increasing labour costs due to Alberta's hot economy. The company announced that it needed to "increase the efficiency of its business."[28] The city of Edmonton had leased 5 hectares (12 acres) of land to Dell at an annual rate of one dollar when the market value of the property amounted to more than

$300,000 a year. Furthermore, Dell enjoyed $400,000 in municipal tax breaks during its three years of operation in the city.[29] Dell did not abandon Edmonton because the company was losing money. In fact, its profits were up over the previous year. Dell abandoned the city because Alberta's hot economy was increasing labour costs, thereby restricting the company's ability to further increase its profits.

Similarly, in February 2008, U.S.-based Convergys announced that it was closing some of its Canadian operations, not because the company was losing money, but because the strong Canadian dollar was inhibiting its efforts to maximize profits. Despite the company's $170 million in profits in 2007, Convergys CEO David Dougherty declared:

> We've got to take some pretty aggressive action to redeploy and move our business to reduce our exposure in some of the key areas where we're being hurt. Most notably we're being hurt today in Canada, and we are taking action to close centres there and move work to other geographies.[30]

In his claim that the company has to take "aggressive action" to increase its profits, it seemed irrelevant to Dougherty that the "geographies" he so callously referred to actually consist of families and communities seeking a measure of economic stability and security.

The Anti-Union Strategy under Neoliberalism

Neoliberal globalization has not only negatively affected the wages of Canadian workers, due to its dismantling of Keynesian-inspired protectionist policies and the Fordist compact; it has also set back labour's right to organize. In reality, many workers have no more right to organize under neoliberalism today than they did when Canada began its industrialization drive a little more than a century ago. After call centres, perhaps the most visible symbol of neoliberalism in the service economy is the U.S.-based retail giant Wal-Mart. Sam Walton opened the first Wal-Mart store in Arkansas in 1962. However, it wasn't until the early 1990s that globalization had established conditions to enable the company to rapidly expand its operations in other countries. Under neoliberal polices implemented by nations in both the North and the South, Wal-Mart not only gained access to foreign markets, but deregulation allowed it to repatriate its profits. The free movement of capital and profits permitted under neoliberalism ensured that U.S.-based executives and shareholders of companies like Wal-Mart could bring "their" money back home.

An important component of Wal-Mart's growth has been China's economic opening and its increasing integration into the global capitalist economy. Wal-Mart has effectively taken advantage of China's massive pool of cheap labour to produce the goods it sells in its stores. Consequently, Wal-Mart is now the world's largest retailer, operating more than 3,500 stores worldwide, employing more than 1.5 million people and generating annual sales of more than $300 billion. In 2005, Wal-Mart earned a record profit of $11.2 billion, which was a 9.4 per cent increase over the previous year.[31]

Wal-Mart's formula for success is to offer retail goods at prices, on average, considerably lower than those of its competitors. The company achieves this through a combination of outsourcing its production to the lowest-cost manufacturer, operating primarily in rural areas where it has less competition, and maintaining wages and benefits considerably below those of its competitors. It has achieved the latter by nurturing an aggressive anti-union stance. Wal-Mart's business model led historian Nelson Lichtenstein to coin the term "Wal-Martization," representing, he believes, the template for 21st-century capitalism. According to Lichtenstein, the Fordist compact that provided benefits to workers in the 20th century has been replaced by a model in which companies offer jobs marked by low wages, short hours, little job security and the denial of collective representation.[32]

Wal-Mart has vigorously pursued a strategy designed to keep the union out and, in those cases where that effort has failed, has attempted to frustrate any attempt by workers to win a collective agreement. In the United States, the United Food and Commercial Workers Union (UFCW) began to target Wal-Mart for organizing and, in 2000, meat cutters in a Jacksonville, Texas store were certified. Within a week the company announced that it was going to shut down its meat-cutting operations and begin purchasing pre-processed meat. This action sent a clear message to Wal-Mart workers throughout the United States that organizing would lead to job loss. All votes on representation since have gone against establishing a union.[33]

Wal-Mart entered Canada in 1994 when it purchased 122 of the country's 144 Woolco stores. By 2008, there were 309 Wal-Mart stores across Canada—including two in CBRM—and the company had become the single largest private employer in the country, with more than 77,000 workers.[34] The first union was organized at a store in Windsor, Ontario, in 1996 and the majority of workers, according to the union, ratified a collective bargaining agreement. However, a group of employees challenged the vote result, contesting the collective agreement in court and preventing it from ever being implemented. The union accused Wal-Mart of manipulating certain employees to sabotage the collective agreement. According to Canadian business professor Roy Adams, "This phenomenon of apparently independent employee groups opposed to unionization has repeatedly appeared in Wal-Mart stores." Adams goes on to note, "One of the results of this effort was that a very labour-unfriendly Conservative Ontario government was prompted to pass legislation taking away the power of the Labour Board to certify unions victimized by illegal activity. The statute came to be known as the Wal-Mart Act."[35]

Despite the setback in Ontario, efforts to unionize continued in other parts of Canada. In December 2003, the UFCW filed a certification application to represent workers at a Wal-Mart store in Jonquière, Quebec. The fact that Quebec was the most pro-union province in Canada—with a 40 per cent unionization rate compared to 29 per cent nationally—posed a greater challenge to Wal-Mart than organizing efforts in other parts of the country. Under Quebec law, a store can be unionized without an employee election if a majority of hourly workers sign union cards. Once the provincial government certifies the signatures, management is obligated to sit down with union representatives to negotiate a collective-bargaining agreement. If an agreement cannot be reached then the provincial government will appoint an arbitrator who can impose a contract.

In response to low pay and poor working conditions, Wal-Mart's pro-union employees in the Jonquière store began lobbying their fellow workers to sign union cards. The store's managers responded by holding mandatory anti-union meetings for employees. Nevertheless, organizers eventually obtained enough signatures, and in August 2004 the store became the only unionized Wal-Mart in North America. Shortly before talks began between management and union representatives to negotiate a collective agreement, Wal-Mart issued a press release announcing that the store was "not meeting its business plan," implying it might have to be closed. Negotiations failed to achieve a collective agreement and, on February 1, 2005, the UFCW applied to the provincial government for arbitration. Eight days later, Wal-Mart announced that it was closing the store.[36] The Jonquière store is the only one that Wal-Mart has ever closed in Canada, and the move illustrates to what length the company is willing to go to prevent its workers from organizing.

The closing of the Jonquière store in Quebec had the desired effect of letting Wal-Mart workers across the country know that they would find themselves unemployed if they organized. Nevertheless, Wal-Mart workers have continued with efforts to organize, although none has yet succeeded and votes to unionize at stores in Windsor, Ontario, in March 2005 and Brossard, Quebec, the following month were defeated badly in the wake of the Jonquière closing. Wal-Mart has responded to the efforts of its workers to organize in much the same way that the capitalist owners of Cape Breton's steel plant and coal mines did one hundred years ago: by harassing pro-union employees, calling on the State to help quash workers' demands and threatening to shut up shop.

Because neoliberalism has established a business-friendly environment that allows companies to easily move their operations anywhere in the world, even those workers who are unionized possess little leverage during contract negotiations. In October 2005, Halifax-based Clearwater Seafoods laid off forty workers at its fish processing plant in North Sydney, Cape Breton, to shift some of its operations to China. Despite the fact that its product was caught in the waters off the coast of Nova Scotia, it proved more profitable for Clearwater to freeze some of the catch and ship it all the way to China, where workers earned 20 cents an hour, than to process the catch in Cape Breton.[37] As Clearwater's CEO Eric Roes made clear, "We must reduce costs and add greater value to the clams we harvest."[38]

Meanwhile, Jackie Evans, a representative of the workers' union, called on the government to protect the processing jobs: "Government cannot allow Clearwater to take Nova Scotia clam and send it to China to be processed. This is taking work away from Nova Scotians so Clearwater can make more money, that doesn't make sense to me."[39] Evans' pleas fell on deaf ears, however, even though the plant was located in the riding of Liberal MP Mark Eyking, who was the parliamentary secretary to the minister of international trade at the time. The government of Prime Minister Paul Martin was, after all, an avid proponent of neoliberalism.

The layoffs suffered by Cape Breton's fish processing workers intensified the hardships endured by a region still reeling from the recent closings of its steel plant and coal mines and the collapse of the cod fisheries. There was more to come. Less than six months after firing the North Sydney workers, Clearwater locked out more than one hundred employees at its Highland Fisheries processing plant in Glace Bay, Cape Breton. The lockout occurred because union negotiators refused to accept a $2.25 an hour pay cut that would have slashed wages to $10.00 an hour—the amount workers earned thirteen years earlier. By having recently laid off workers at its North Sydney operation and shifting those jobs to China, the company had sent a clear message to its employees at Highland Fisheries: accept the pay cut or lose your jobs. Effectively, under globalization, the large pool of surplus labour providing leverage for capitalist elites during wage negotiations is no longer outside the factory gates, but half way around the world. The Highland Fisheries workers remained locked out for more than a year before finally capitulating and accepting the wage cut along with a reduction in health- and life-insurance benefits.[40]

In previous capitalist eras, wages were often linked to profits. In other words, when a company was profitable, often the wages of workers would increase or at least remain constant. Conversely, when companies were losing money, workers would have to accept pay cuts or be laid off. Under neoliberalism, this economic logic has been turned on its head; deregulation and the free movement of goods and capital have rendered workers all but impotent. Many companies are forcing workers to accept pay cuts and are even firing employees at the same time they are reporting substantial, even re-cord, profits. One month before locking out the Highland Fisheries workers, Clearwater announced it had earned $21 million in profits the previous year.[41] And yet, despite its profitability, the company demanded that its workers accept an 18-per-cent pay cut.

Many other companies in the neoliberal era have sought to in-crease profits by cutting labour costs. They have often achieved the downsizing of their labour forces through the outsourcing of jobs to lower-paying and non-unionized companies. Nowhere has this been more evident in Canada than in the country's largest telecommunications company, BCE, which owns Bell Canada, Internet provider Sympatico, and Bell ExpressVu satellite television service. In February 2006, BCE stunned its workforce when it announced that it would lay off between 3,000 and 4,000 workers. The layoffs were announced only a year after the company had cut 5,000 jobs. Did BCE fire more than 8,000 workers because it was losing money? Did it dismiss them because the company, while still in the black, was concerned about declining profits? In fact, neither of those two scenarios applied to BCE. The company earned an impressive $1.9 billion in profits in 2005, up from $1.5 billion the previous year.[42] The workers were fired so that BCE could become "more competitive," which is little more than a euphemism for "even more profitable."

Canada's Energy Policies in the Era of Free Trade

It is not only the service sector that has been a primary contributor to Canada's economic growth under neoliberalism, but also the energy industry. However, Canada's oil wealth has not contributed to the country becoming more energy self-sufficient. To the contrary, neoliberal policies have resulted in Canada becoming the leading supplier of oil to the United States, while increasing its own dependence on Middle Eastern oil.

In 1980, the government of Prime Minister Pierre Trudeau implemented the National Energy Program (NEP), which called for an increased role for state-owned Petro-Canada in oil production. The objective of the NEP was to make Canada more energy self-sufficient, regulate domestic oil prices to avoid global market fluctuations, give preferential treatment to Canadian companies, and increase the government's revenues from petroleum production. Not surprisingly, Alberta vehemently opposed the NEP because it redistributed the province's oil revenues across Canada. The NEP only lasted six years because Prime Minister Mulroney's neoliberal reforms terminated the program.

Under neoliberalism, Canada has been far from energy self-sufficient. It produced 3.1 million barrels of oil a day in 2006, while consuming 2.2 million barrels, suggesting that it could in fact be self-sufficient in oil.[43] But it exported 2.3 million barrels a day of its domestic production to the United States that year, thereby requiring it to purchase almost a million barrels a day from the global market, primarily from the Middle East, South America and Norway.[44] In other words, Canada exported 74 per cent of its oil production to the United States in 2006 while importing 63 per cent of the oil it consumed. As a result, Canada has supplanted Saudi Arabia as the number-one supplier of oil to the United States and is now more reliant on Middle Eastern oil than its neighbour to the south.

The North American Free Trade Agreement (NAFTA) has played a significant role in undermining Canadian energy sovereignty. NAFTA ensures that should a global oil crisis arise, Canada cannot reduce its exports to the United States to cope with its own demand. Under article 605(a), also known as the "proportionality clause," Canada is prohibited from reducing oil exports as a share of the country's production to below "the proportion prevailing in the most recent 36-month period for which data are available."[45] In other words, in the event of a crisis, Canada must continue to export to the United States the same percentage—74 per cent in 2006—of its total oil production as in the three years before the crisis, while scrambling to obtain oil from the global market to meet its own needs. Additionally, article 605(b) prohibits Canada from imposing an export tax on the oil it supplies to the United States unless it applies the same level of taxation to Canadians.[46]

Neoliberal policies have also led to oil companies paying royalty rates that are among the lowest in the world. Companies operating in Alberta's oil sands—which account for 45 per cent of Canada's oil production—pay 1 per cent in royalties on their production, a rate lower than applied to conventional crude, because of the high costs involved in extracting oil from the tar-like substance.[47] In contrast, the government of President Hugo Chávez in Venezuela, which has challenged neoliberal doctrine, increased royalty rates in 2001 from 1 per cent to 16.6 per cent on the heavy crude produced in the Orinoco basin—where production costs are comparable to those of the Alberta oil sands—and further raised them in 2006 to 33.3 per cent.[48]

Additionally, the Venezuelan state oil company (Petróleos de Venezuela S.A., PDVSA) owns a majority share in all extraction operations, which means that it owns at least 50 per cent of the oil produced in each field. Sixty-seven per cent of PDVSA's earnings are turned over to the national government, which spends much of it on social programs to ensure that the Venezuelan people are garnering a significant share of the national wealth generated by oil. Since Petro-Canada was privatized under neoliberalism, Canada no longer has a state oil company and, as a result, private energy companies—more than half of which are American—own 100 per cent of the oil produced in Canada.

Private companies not only own all of the oil in Canada and pay low royalties, they also receive massive tax breaks. The Pembina Institute reports that since 1996, oil companies operating in Canada have enjoyed tax breaks amounting to an average of $1.4 billion annually.[49] According to a 2007 report by the Council of Canadians, the Norwegian government received 88 per cent of the country's oil revenues through royalties and corporate income tax from 1995 to 2002. In contrast, the province of Alberta only pocketed 50 per cent of its oil earnings.[50] As a result of lower royalty and corporate income tax rates, oil and gas companies operating in Canada enjoyed an average net profit margin of 14 per cent, compared with the 8.2 per cent earned by the world's nine largest energy companies in all operations outside of Canada.[51]

It is difficult to understand why Canada would give such enormous tax breaks to companies in an era of record-high oil prices. Production costs in Alberta's oil sands run about $25 a barrel, while the global market price for oil was more than $100 a barrel for much of 2008. As a result of high oil prices, companies operating in the oil sands earned record profits. For example, U.S.-based ExxonMobil reported $40 billion in earnings for 2007, the largest profit in history for a U.S. corporation.[52] Such exorbitant profit margins raise the question: Do these companies really need to be subsidized by Canadian taxpayers?

Companies operating in Alberta's oil sands have benefited not only from the economic conditions established under neoliberalism, but also from lax environmental policies. Two of Canada's top six single sources of greenhouse gas emissions are located in the oil sands: the operations of Syncrude and Suncor Energy.[53] Even more troubling is the fact that production in the oil sands is supposed to escalate dramatically over the next decade, from its current rate of more than one million barrels a day to three million barrels. More greenhouse gases will be emitted by the oil sands of Fort McMurray which has a population of 61,000, than by the entire country of Denmark, with its 5.4 million, by 2015.[54] Furthermore, producing a single barrel of oil requires an average of four barrels of water, while the southern part of the province regularly endures drought conditions.[55] In fact, water allocations to the oil sands operations double those to the city of Calgary.[56] And while Canadians endure the environmental devastation wrought by the oil sands, most of the oil goes to serve the energy needs of the United States.

The situation regarding energy sovereignty is much the same in Atlantic Canada. All eastbound oil pipelines from Alberta terminate in Ontario or Quebec. As a result, 90 per cent of the oil consumed in Atlantic Canada is imported, primarily from the Middle East, South America and Norway.[57] The region relies on these imports despite the fact that it produces significant quantities of oil and natural gas, primarily in offshore fields in Nova Scotia and Newfoundland. As in Alberta, oil companies have benefited from favourable terms in their deals to exploit Atlantic Canada's offshore oil and gas reserves. In oil operations off the coast of Newfoundland, companies pay 53 per cent in royalties to the federal and provincial governments—21 per cent and 32 per cent, respectively.[58] This amount stands in stark contrast to that in Norway, which, as previously mentioned, retains 88 per cent of its oil revenues.

Instead of using its own reserves to meet its own needs, the energy strategy of Nova Scotia's provincial government has focused on the exploitation of offshore oil and gas for export to the United States. Newfoundland, by contrast, has recently sought to capture a greater share of its offshore oil and gas wealth, despite objections by energy companies. In an attempt to increase his province's share of oil wealth, Newfoundland Premier Danny Williams has sought to obtain part-ownership for the province of future energy ventures, beginning with the undeveloped Hebron oil project. In a clear illustration of its neoliberal philosophy, the Harper government refused to back Williams in his battle against the oil companies, including ExxonMobil and ChevronTexaco, arguing that "[f]ederal intervention in this type of commercial arrangement would be inconsistent with the market principles the Government of Canada is promoting."[59] Nevertheless, Williams persevered in his attempt to ensure that Newfoundlanders received a greater share of their natural resource wealth and, in August 2007, announced that the province would own a 4.9-per-cent share in the Hebron project and a 10-per-cent stake in future projects—in addition to the province's share of royalties.[60] Williams is also seeking legislation that would allow the province to repossess any oil and gas fields left fallow by energy companies for an as-yet-undetermined "unreasonable" amount of time. In their attempts to criticize and insult the Newfoundland premier, neoliberal advocates have compared him to the "business-unfriendly" Venezuelan president Hugo Chávez, who has increased the amount of oil wealth retained by his government to fund social programs, particularly health care and education.[61]

The Social Fallout

The expansion of the service sector, along with dramatic increases in oil production, has contributed to impressive economic growth in Canada, thanks to business-friendly policies implemented under the mantra of neoliberalism. But who is benefiting from this economic growth? Who is pocketing the wealth generated? Politicians, economists and the mainstream media have repeatedly reminded the public that Canada's economy is booming and that the government is achieving impressive surpluses year after year. Naturally, the implication of these achievements is that Canadians are doing great. But in reality, the standard of living of most Canadians has actually declined in the era of globalization.

As has occurred in the global South, the gap between the rich and the poor in Canada has increased under neoliberalism. During the 1980s, before the implementation of the U.S.-Canada free trade agreement, average disposable income increased for Canadian households in all income groups. Furthermore, disposable income grew at a greater rate for the poorest 20 per cent of the population than for other income groups during the decade, thereby narrowing the income gap between rich and poor, and increasing equality. In every province, the income gap was less in 1990 than in 1980.[62] For much of the 1980s, Keynesian policies, the Fordist compact and the welfare state all remained relatively intact with the shift to neoliberalism not occurring until the latter part of the decade.

A May 2007 Statistics Canada report draws a similar conclusion on growing income equality during the 1980s and notes increased inequality in the neoliberal era. According to the report, "family income became more equally distributed across the 1980s. [...] However, from 1989 to 2004, income inequality rose."[63] The report goes on to point out that, between 1989 and 2004, after-tax income for the poorest 10 per cent of Canadians declined by 8 per cent while the richest 10 per cent saw their income increase by 24 per cent. As a result, the income gap between the richest Canadians and the poorest increased by 35 per cent during that period.[64] The report also notes that the growing inequality coincided with the dismantling of the Keynesian policy framework, as this shift "occurred at the same time as a reduction in the generosity of several income transfer programs, including the Employment Insurance and Social Assistance Programs," and that it "potentially reflects a weakening of the redistributive role of the Canadian state."[65]

The Statistics Canada report also illustrates how neoliberalism has benefited corporations and hurt workers. It notes that workers saw a 6 per cent decline in their share of Canada's national income between 1989 and 2005. Meanwhile, corporations experienced a 5 per cent rise in their share of the income pie during the same period due to increased profits.[66] Ultimately, the report makes evident that the rich have gotten richer and the poor have become poorer under globalization. And yet, despite the growing income inequality, federal tax cuts implemented in 2001 disproportionately benefited wealthier Canadians. Canadians earning less than $30,000 a year only received a 1 per cent income tax cut, while those earning between $60,000 and $100,000 enjoyed a 3 per cent reduction in their tax rate.[67]

A study by economists Emmanuel Saez and Michael R. Veall that looks at the evolution of high incomes in North America analyzes the trajectory of the earnings of the wealthy over a much longer period of time. By studying the period from 1920 to 2000, Saez and Veall allow us to draw comparisons between particular economic models and the income earned by the wealthiest 5 per cent of the population. The study shows that from 1920 to 1940—the tail end of the liberal capitalist era—the richest 5 per cent of Canadians earned between 30 and 40 per cent of the national income. Their income plummeted during the Second World War and in 1945 stood at 25 per cent of the national total. It saw a further decline in the postwar decades, eventually bottoming out at 22 per cent in 1986—the period most predominantly marked by Keynesian policies and the Fordist compact. However, within a couple of years of the Mulroney government launching its neoliberal overhaul of Canada's economy, the income earned by the wealthiest 5 per cent of Canadians took a sharp turn upward, and by 2000 they were earning 29 per cent of the national income.[68] The study makes clear that the liberal and neoliberal eras were marked by higher levels of inequality than the Keynesian period.

Saez and Veall show that the same recovery enjoyed in the neoliberal era by the wealthiest 5 per cent of income earners in Canada also occurred in the United States and Britain, but not to the same degree in France and the Canadian province of Quebec. The authors suggest that the principal cause was wage pressure at the high end of the scale in the United States, which forced companies in English-speaking Canada and Britain to become more competitive to avoid a brain drain.[69] Curiously, Saez and Veall fail to also draw the obvious comparisons between income levels and the prevalent economic model during any given period of the study. For instance, neoliberalism has been implemented to a greater degree in the United States, English-speaking Canada and Britain than in France and Quebec, where unions remain strong and the welfare state has survived relatively intact, thereby restricting the ability of the rich to significantly increase their income share.

An important indicator of how neoliberalism and its resulting increase in inequality have negatively impacted Canada's poor is child poverty rates. Between 1989 and 1999, in Atlantic Canada, child poverty increased by 38.4 per cent in Prince Edward Island (to 17.3 per cent of all children), 29.8 per cent in Newfoundland (to 25.7 per cent), 12.4 per cent in Nova Scotia (to 18.1 per cent) and 0.6 per cent in New Brunswick (to 18.0 per cent).[70] Although the gap between the rich and the poor has been growing, and increasing numbers of children have been forced to endure poverty, the federal government has made it more difficult for those in need to access unemployment insurance, health care, education and other social programs, through stricter eligibility requirements and reductions in funding. In the Chrétien government's 1995 budget, for example, finance minister Paul Martin slashed federal cash payments to the provinces for health care, social programs and post-secondary education by an unprecedented 40 per cent.[71]

Neoliberals claim that cutbacks in social spending are necessary to achieve fiscal discipline. However, since the late 1990s, the federal government has gone way beyond achieving fiscal discipline, generating massive surpluses averaging almost $10 billion annually. While some of the surplus revenue has gone to paying down the national debt, neoliberal ideology has also driven the handling of the remainder of the money. Rather than increase funding for health care, education or other social programs, the Harper government has preferred to distribute the money to individual Canadians through sales and income tax cuts. In his first two years in office, Prime Minister Stephen Harper implemented two consecutive 1-per-cent reductions in the Goods and Services Tax (GST) as a way of redistributing some of the federal surplus to individuals, rather than using the money to boost social spending, particularly in the areas of health care and education.

The intentional underfunding of the health care system over the past fifteen years—particularly in the aforementioned budget of finance minister Paul Martin—has created problems, such as long wait times and a shortage of doctors. The shortcomings of the public health care system have provided neoliberals with the opportunity to promote privatization as a solution. One institution pushing it is the right-wing Atlantic Institute for Market Studies (AIMS). This think tank receives significant funding from corporations and is a leading proponent of neoliberalism, not only in the Atlantic provinces, but across Canada—as evidenced by the fact that the institute's president, Brian Lee Crowley, took a leave of absence to become an economic advisor to Prime Minister Harper. AIMS has promoted increased private-sector participation in the health care system as a solution to long wait times and doctor shortages. In his paper, titled "The Potential of Private Sector Health Care in Canada," Brian Ferguson of AIMS suggests that solving Canada's health care problems would require "permitting greater private, as in non-government, sector involvement in the way Medicare operates."[72] Ferguson refers to shortcomings in Britain's National Health Service (NHS) to illustrate how people prefer private health care insurance to an inadequate public system:

> There is one circumstance that will prompt people to switch to private insurance, and that is when they begin to doubt that the public system will be there when they need it. Recent evidence

from the UK indicates that as waiting times under the NHS increased, people tended to switch to private insurance (and private supply) not necessarily to jump the queue, but because the longer waiting times signaled a decline in the quality of NHS care and a reduction in the probability that the public system would be there when they needed it. Dissatisfaction with the quality of the NHS seems to be a significant factor in prompting people to buy private insurance.[73]

While it might not be surprising that people would choose private health care over a failing public system, Ferguson fails to point out that the NHS had become inadequate because Prime Minister Margaret Thatcher intentionally ran the public health care system into the ground. The undermining of the NHS through the implementation of neoliberal policies in the 1980s was intended to lay the groundwork for the proposal of partial or full privatization as a solution. Ferguson does, however, begrudgingly acknowledge that recent efforts by the British government to improve the NHS—in response to public demand—have "reversed the trend, prompting individuals who had gone private to come back to the public system."[74]

Similarly, in Canada, the insufficient health care funding provided by Ottawa to provincial governments has undermined the public system. As a result, Canada has the lowest doctor-patient ratio of any industrialized nation—2.2 per 1,000 Canadians. One of the problems, according to Dr. Brian Day, president of the Canadian Medical Association, is that Canada's medical schools are not producing enough doctors. Meanwhile, 11 per cent of those students who do graduate from the country's medical schools go on to practice medicine in the United States.[75]

While neoliberals repeatedly claim that "throwing money at the problem" is not the solution, an argument could be made that throwing money at this particular problem would contribute significantly to increasing the number of doctors and decreasing wait times. For example, additional funding for medical schools in order to help increase enrolments would result in more doctors. Furthermore, by increasing the salaries of doctors, the government would reduce some of the incentive for Canadian doctors to practice in the United States. While this is a market-related solution, it is crucial in the current global capitalist context, given Canada's close geographic proximity to the United States, which makes the Canadian public health care system particularly vulnerable to a brain drain. Yet another incentive would be for the government to cover the costs of medical school for doctors who commit to practicing medicine in Canada for at least ten years following graduation. Furthermore, increased funding to build new or to expand existing facilities would resolve the shortage of hospital beds.

Neoliberals claim that such initiatives to improve the public health care system would place too heavy a fiscal burden on the government. However, according to Prime Minister Harper, a 1-per-cent cut in the GST—half of his total reduction—reduced government revenues by $6 billion.[76] This amount of government revenue could have gone a long way toward improving the health care system for all Canadians. However, the Harper government instead chose to continue with its adherence to neoliberal doctrine and to further undermine the viability of public health care.

Rather than adequately funding public health care, neoliberals instead promote a dual system that would allow private health care for those who can afford it and a public system for the rest. For many neoliberals, the two-tiered proposal is simply a strategy for getting the private sector's foot in the door. Once Canadians have been convinced to accept a role for the private sector, neoliberals would then likely begin pushing to completely privatize health care. Inevitably, a privatized health care system would put itself beyond the reach of many Canadians, particularly the working poor, the most prevalent sector among the estimated forty-seven million people who lack health insurance in the United States.[77] And even if a semblance of a public system were retained for those who could not afford private health coverage, it would most likely also result in a two-tiered system in the quality of care.

The neoliberal strategy being applied to public health care is also undermining Canada's post-secondary education system. Canadians attending university are finding that—even without privatization—federal cuts in funding have made the cost of obtaining a post-secondary education increasingly expensive. In 2007, the average annual cost for undergraduate tuition in Canada was $4,524, which represented a dramatic increase from $1,185 in 1988. In Nova Scotia, the combination of pro-neoliberal federal and provincial governments has resulted in students paying the highest tuition rates in the country—an average of $6,422 a year in 2007.[78] To cope with reduced federal and provincial funding for post-secondary education, universities have had to raise tuition rates, as well as increasingly turning to corporations for funding. By creating programs to attract corporate funds, universities have shifted away from their traditional role of providing a well-rounded education to their students. As sociologist William I. Robinson has argued:

> Over the past decades, and in tandem with the spread of capitalist globalization, we have witnessed relentless pressures worldwide to commodify higher education, the increasing privatization of universities and their penetration by transnational corporate capital. If the university is to pull back from such a course it must fulfill a larger social function in the interests of broad publics and from the vantage point of a social logic that is inevitably at odds with the corporate logic of global capitalism.[79]

While some universities have willingly engaged with corporations, others have sought such funding as a matter of survival. As a result of the penetration of corporate capital described by Robinson, some components of university curricula amount to little more than corporate training programs. In 2001, for example, Cape Breton University signed a multi-year agreement with ExxonMobil to provide training in petroleum engineering to the oil company's Russian and Angolan workers. The fact that ExxonMobil is paying Cape Breton University to provide its workers with specific "training" rather than a broader "education" is apparent in the language used by representatives of both the oil company and the university. According to Alex Dodds, president of ExxonMobil Canada, "[t]he ExxonMobil employees from Angola and Russia who have participated in this program have received excellent *training* which they will draw on when they return to their home countries" (emphasis added), while John Harker, president of Cape Breton University, announced: "Congratulations to the second graduating class from this international *training* program with ExxonMobil. We continue to illustrate through the success of these international programs that our *training* is world class" (emphasis added).[80]

Similarly, St. Mary's University in Halifax, Nova Scotia, established the Investment Management of Portfolios in Atlantic Canada Training Program (IMPACT) in 2004. As the program's title makes clear, IMPACT provides "training" to business students interested in careers in financial investment. According to the university, IM-

PACT is funded by "a generous anonymous donation" and could not "succeed without significant involvement from the professional investment community."[81] The board of directors overseeing the program comprises individuals from the university's Sobey School of Business, as well as outside investment professionals. In fact, as part of their training, the students "make investment decisions as a team, with the guidance of industry mentors" from some of the largest investment companies in Canada.[82] In other words, the students receive hands-on training from corporate professionals and according to David Wicks, dean of the Sobey School of Business, "This type of experiential learning is an important component of the future path of higher education."[83]

The "training" role of universities is in line with the neoliberal view of post-secondary education and, in order to better achieve its desired objective, the Atlantic Institute of Market Studies advocates privatizing all the universities in Atlantic Canada. A report on education titled "From Public U to Private U: An Atlantic Canadian Opportunity," published by AIMS in 2005, claims that the problem with public universities is that they are "sheltered from the accountability that market forces impose." The solution, according to AIMS, is a "return to the concept of the truly 'private' university, whether run on a 'for-profit' or 'not-for-profit' basis." Furthermore, notes the conservative think-tank, the "first university that deliberately takes this step would have a major marketing advantage in Canada and first-mover status with regard to corporate and private philanthropy."[84]

As the report makes evident, the process of privatization has already begun, as cuts in public funding have resulted in tuition accounting for a higher percentage of operating costs than government grants for many universities. In its report, AIMS describes a potential transition process to complete privatization:

> The financial implications of moving to a truly private model are relatively simple in the first instance: how to replace the annual operating grant. One direct route would be an infusion to the endowment of $300–500 million or more. The more likely alternative would be to raise tuition levels to the $10,000–13,000 per year level—a practical and possible route to privatization that would likely be highly rewarded in both the marketplace and philanthropic circles.[85]

The report fails to point out that those "philanthropic circles" would primarily consist of corporations and the universities most likely to receive such endowments would be those who best serve corporate interests. Any institution and academic departments that seriously question the neoliberal paradigm or the hegemony of the marketplace in society are likely to find themselves marginalized and desperately scrambling for funding to survive, which is the economic reality for most progressive non-profit organizations under neoliberalism. Furthermore, the doubling of tuition fees recommended by AIMS would represent a return to the days when children of the nation's elites were the only ones who had access to higher education.

A serious flaw—from a societal perspective, not a neoliberal one—in the AIMS report is its failure to ask the fundamental question about what the role of a university should be. For instance, should universities be obligated to provide an affordable, well-rounded education that helps students better understand the world in which they live and provides them with the necessary tools to raise important philosophical questions about their lives and society? Or should universities be responsible for little more than preparing students for a career? The AIMS report accepts the latter point of view as a given. The institute also unquestioningly assumes that an education that serves the needs of the marketplace is good for society as a whole. In reality, however, a university system primarily funded by corporations would most likely only serve the interests of corporations. After all, while corporations would willingly provide funding for business, science, engineering and technology programs, they would be far less likely to support the social sciences and the arts to the same degree.

In contrast to Canada's approach, governments in Scandinavian nations have decided to maintain the philosophy of affordable education as a human right. In fact, in Sweden, not only is university education still free, but full-time students also receive a monthly stipend from the government to help cover their living costs.[86] Furthermore, maintaining such high levels of social spending has not diminished the quality of life enjoyed by the average Swede. In fact, in the United Nations 2006 Human Development Index, which analyzes education, health care and purchasing power to determine quality of life, Sweden ranked fourth in the world, two places above

Canada.[87] One could argue that the Swedes enjoy a higher quality of life, not despite the country's social policies, but because of them. The comparison with Sweden makes evident that the Canadian government's cutbacks in spending on post-secondary education are ideologically driven policy decisions rather than "necessary" or "inevitable" fiscal policy. After all, Sweden exists in the same context of global capitalism as Canada.

Political Scientist David Johnson has illustrated just how easy it would be to provide free post-secondary education to Canadians by pointing out that the $6 billion in annual revenue that the government relinquished with its initial 1-per-cent cut in the GST would cover the tuition costs of every university student in the country.[88] However, such a policy initiative would run contrary to the neoliberal agenda of the Harper government.

As a result of rising costs of post-secondary education, Canadian university students have been forced to incur increasingly high levels of debt. This situation has been particularly severe in post-industrial communities like Cape Breton, where families already struggling economically are often unable to contribute money to help cover their children's tuition fees. Not only are increasing numbers of Canadians burdened with large student-loan debts, but overall debt has also increased dramatically under neoliberalism. Between 1990 and 2007, the average debt load for Canadians increased by 54 per cent and now stands at $80,100.[89] While home mortgages and car loans account for a significant percentage of the debt load, the average credit card debt constitutes an ever higher portion, almost doubling from $11,955 in 1990 to $22,500 in 2007.[90] Perhaps most troubling is the fact that the higher levels of credit card debt has not primarily resulted from purchases of large-ticket items, but rather from more and more families having to borrow money to make ends meet. In fact, 52 per cent of Canadian adults claim they have to borrow money just to meet day-to-day expenses.[91] In part, the increased debt loads carried by Canadians have resulted from the fact that two incomes in a household often prove insufficient to support a family, particularly when those incomes are derived from low-paying service sector jobs.

The long-term sustainability of the neoliberal model is also threatened by the difficulties many Canadians face in saving for retirement. Under neoliberalism, the burden of having an adequate pension has shifted to the individual because the government pension is insufficient. However, the combination of higher debt loads and increasing numbers of low-paid service sector jobs has made it difficult for many workers to set aside money for their so-called golden years. In 1990, Canadians saved an average of $7,500 a year, but this amount had plummeted to only $1,000 a year by 2007.[92] And in 2005, according to Statistics Canada, 29 per cent of Canadian families and 45.2 per cent of unattached individuals had no private pension assets. The situation is particularly dire for the working poor, as 64 per cent of families with an income of less than $30,000 have no pension savings.[93] What will happen to these Canadians when they retire and cannot afford to support themselves?

The Failure of Community Economic Development

Many in Cape Breton have responded to neoliberalism by seeking to further integrate themselves into the economic system that caused their problems in the first place: global capitalism. The acceptance of provincial, national and international neoliberal structures by local development leaders has meant that most so-called alternative projects have amounted to little more than exercises in survival economics. Local politicians and community leaders herald the creation of jobs related to the opening of a new box store or call centre and claim that Cape Breton's economic situation is improving. In reality, unemployed Cape Bretoners reluctantly fill jobs that pay poverty-level wages because anything is better than nothing. Acquiescence to the neoliberal doctrine by local and national political elites has ensured that British Prime Minister Margaret Thatcher's catchphrase—"there is no alternative"—has become a reality.

Attempts by elected officials and community leaders to resolve economic problems on a local level without simultaneously challenging the national and international contexts of these issues often fail to establish sustainable alternatives. Nowhere is this more evident than in Cape Breton. In reality, Cape Breton's economic problems, both historically and today, have resulted from a combination of local and outside factors. Logically then, economic solutions must take into account both factors. However, most of the economic development initiatives in post-industrial Cape Breton are government driven and, because of the neoliberal propensities of the provincial and federal governments, promote neoliberal principles, particularly the focus on achieving economic growth.

Enterprise Cape Breton Corporation (ECBC) is a Crown corporation that was established in 1987 as the successor to the Industrial Development Division, which had in turn been established 20 years earlier. ECBC's mission has been to diversify Cape Breton's economy, steering it away from its reliance on steel production and coal mining. ECBC has funded community-based projects such as Cape Breton Power—a wind energy cooperative that is forced under provincial regulations to sell the electricity it generates to NSP—and the Sydney farmers' market. Such projects, according to ECBC's director of communications D. A. Landry, reflect the corporation's 1960s-era mandate, which has never been modified and is unlikely to be found in any Crown development organization that might be established today.[94] However, despite ECBC's Keynesian roots and continuing support for certain community-based projects, the corporation has increasingly adhered to the federal government's pro-neoliberal line in recent years. Instead of making increased self-sufficiency and sustainability in Cape Breton its primary focus, ECBC has emphasized the promotion of private business growth rooted in the neoliberal principle applied to most periphery locales, which calls for increased exports and deeper integration into the global economy. ECBC's neoliberal leanings are evident in the guidelines listed for some of its programs. For example, it provides funding to businesses seeking to implement "innovation projects" because "ECBC recognizes that to be competitive in the global economy business must innovate to improve or develop new products and services." ECBC also provides funding to the island's boat-building sector, although it "must be demonstrated that the costs are being incurred for the purpose of servicing export sales opportunities."[95] In a seemingly contradictory stance, ECBC requires that its partners and funding recipients ensure their business plans are sustainable at the same time it pushes them towards greater integration with an increasingly unpredictable and unreliable global economy.

ECBC has also provided generous subsidies to U.S.-based call centre companies such as Stream, EDS and Upsource to encourage them set up shop in Cape Breton. Additionally, ECBC has provided funding for a luxury resort for wealthy foreigners who are more than capable of covering the project's costs. In early 2008, it was announced that ECBC would provide more than $1 million in funding for the Louisbourg Resort Golf and Spa, despite earlier assurances that no taxpayers' dollars would be used for the development. The resort will have up to 400 houses priced between $400,000 and $1 million, with most expected to be purchased as second homes by wealthy Europeans. While proponents for the project claim that the luxury homes will contribute significantly to the municipality's property tax base, they fail to note that it will also drive up property values and, by extension, taxes for many Cape Bretoners who cannot afford to pay them.[96] Other economic development organizations such as the public-private funded Cape Breton County Economic Development Authority (CBCEDA) have promoted the same neoliberal-influenced development model as ECBC.

Another development approach used in Cape Breton has been that of community economic development (CED). According to sociologist Scott MacAuley, CED initiatives differ from those pushed by government agencies in that they ideally advocate a participatory approach to meeting a community's economic needs. In other words, the members of the community become the primary political and economic decision-makers. According to MacAuley:

> Taking these aims seriously suggests the counter-hegemonic potential that is inherent in CED. A community economic development approach which aims to meet the needs of all the people and to do so in a way that is participatory counters the logic of capitalist development which prioritizes profit over need and which limits participation in economic development decision-making to those who own the means of production.[97]

In reality, however, few CED organizations function that way. Instead, they operate more like corporations, which is exactly how they refer to themselves. Cape Breton's New Dawn Enterprises is Canada's oldest CED corporation, and it likens itself to the Antigonish Movement. But New Dawn's version of CED in the neoliberal era is not reminiscent of the model espoused by its famous predecessor, which promoted citizens' cooperatives. According to sociologist Constance deRoche, "New Dawn's mode of leadership differs from that of the Antigonish Movement, which worked to activate the masses. New Dawn is not especially interested in the ordinary citizen."[98] In fact, New Dawn is a non-profit corporation that owns several for-profit business subsidiaries operating in the areas of housing and health care services. Being a non-profit corporation, New Dawn reinvests all profits earned by its CED projects, in existing programs or other new and profitable endeavours.

According to Rankin MacSween, president of New Dawn, the corporation has sought to achieve economic development and to address certain social problems through locally owned and operated private sector initiatives. While he acknowledges that the government has a responsibility to address social problems, such as housing shortages for low-income families, by providing funding and other support, MacSween believes that locally based third-sector organizations such as New Dawn are best situated to handle the actual delivery and management of such services. Reflecting a distrust of governmental micro-management that is rooted in the provincial and federal governments' painfully drawn-out closure of the unprofitable coal and steel sectors in Cape Breton, MacSween argues that "government shouldn't be in the retail business, it should be in the wholesale business. And the government was involved in the retail business in Cape Breton for too long and we suffered because of it."[99]

MacAuley, however, claims that there is a fundamental contradiction between the business methods on which New Dawn relies and its stated objective to address social problems within the community. New Dawn's need to earn profits to sustain itself as a corporation results in its bottom line heavily influencing economic and social development decisions, rather than the most critical needs of the community. So while New Dawn addresses certain needs in the community, its capacity, as MacAuley points out, "is limited by its acceptance of capitalist hegemony and its dependence on business enterprises that must prioritize the needs of capital."[100]

Sociologist deRoche has also noted that many community economic development corporations implement projects that acquiesce to neoliberal doctrine rather than challenge it. In other words, they have accepted that the welfare of people should be left to the private sector, whether "for-profit" or "non-profit." Furthermore, while many advocates and practitioners of this CED model in Cape Breton criticize traditional dependency theory, they simultaneously suggest that the island maintains a "culture of dependency," where people are incapable of exhibiting any significant sense of agency in order to solve their own problems. According to deRoche:

The culture-of-dependency perspective is consonant with the new post-Fordist rhetoric that excuses entrenched authorities from public responsibility, places disadvantaged people at the mercy of market forces and charity, and leaves community-based ventures to struggle to create opportunities. In the context of power structures that offer only Hobson's choices (i.e., between equally unsatisfactory alternatives, in effect, no choice at all), third-sector institutions may serve to ease post-Fordist dislocations, and thus be welcome. But their champions should not add insult to injury by blaming the victims of post-industrialism for their unenviable position.[101]

In reality, Cape Bretoners—as workers' struggles over the past century have repeatedly illustrated—possess a significant degree of agency and have not simply been passive recipients of the consequences of external factors. However, they have often had to endure the negative fallout resulting from these external factors, despite their protestations and efforts to develop alternatives.

The Need to Challenge Global Structures

The new economy in the global North has shifted a significant portion of the workforce out of well-paid, unionized industrial jobs and into the low-paid, non-unionized service sector. Capitalist elites have portrayed this economic transition to neoliberalism as an inevitable evolution of capitalism when, in reality, it is the result of conscious, ideologically driven policies. The driving force behind these policies has been the capitalist imperative to increase profits, regardless of the social and economic consequences borne by a majority of the population. These consequences have proven to be severe in Canada, as evidenced by increasing inequality, deteriorating health care and rising tuition costs for post-secondary education, among other things. As a result, more and more Canadians are beginning to search for alternatives to a neoliberal paradigm that is not working for them. However, local initiatives seeking to function within the structures of the new economic order have failed to provide sustainable alternatives, as evidenced by CED efforts in Cape Breton.

Ultimately, local economies cannot be de-linked from the global economic system, particularly in this era of neoliberal globalization. Local initiatives must simultaneously challenge neoliberalism at the local, national and international levels to achieve broader structural changes in order to establish a sustainable political and economic model amenable to local, democratic decision-making. A failure to implement broad structural changes will ensure that local efforts continually fail to respond to the most powerful causes of the social and economic problems plaguing post-industrial communities like Cape Breton. As deRoche points out, "Grassroots strivings must be understood in the context of power imbalances that are characteristic of globalization, and local cultural perspectives must be understood in the framework of pan-systemic forces that include neo-liberal ideology."[102]

Four

Alternatives to Global Capitalism

Attempts from within the capitalist paradigm to address the social and economic inequalities caused by the model have proven only moderately successful at best. As previously discussed, inequality increased during the liberal and neoliberal eras and was only partially reduced under the Keynesian policy framework during the middle decades of the 20th century. Even during the Keynesian era, half the world's population endured poverty and, despite increased regulation, global capitalism's assault on the environment still proved relentless.

Capitalist elites have constantly resisted any efforts to redistribute "their" wealth. They dismantled the Keynesian policy framework at the first opportunity to increase profits, regardless of the social and environmental consequences in both the global North and the global South. Throughout the world, neoliberalism has undermined health care, education and other social programs that benefit significant portions of the population. In Cape Breton, local communities have been rendered powerless to address the social and economic consequences of neoliberalism because most of the policy decisions affecting their lives are made in the distant cities of Halifax and Ottawa. Likewise in Colombia, where much of the population is opposed to neoliberalism, people can do little to restructure the model as long as the country's political and economic elites remain willing to abide by the rules laid down by U.S.-dominated international institutions, such as the IMF and the World Bank.

Capitalist elites in both Canada and Colombia have ensured that regulatory and legal structures on both the national and international levels work to their own benefit while simultaneously restricting the autonomy of communities to establish more democratic, egalitarian and sustainable alternatives to capitalism. In fact, the governments of Canada and Colombia have negotiated a bilateral free trade agreement to further entrench the neoliberal model in both nations. The agreement provides a clear illustration of how the Canadian government's pro-corporate policies are out of step with the views of the majority of Canadians. In a July 2007 poll, 73 per cent of Canadians said their federal government should not negotiate free trade agreements with countries that have dubious human rights records.[1] The same month, Prime Minister Harper responded to criticism of his free trade negotiations with Colombia, the country with the worst human rights record in the hemisphere, by stating: "We're not going to say, 'Fix all your social, political and human-rights problems, and only then will we engage in trade relations with you.' That's a ridiculous position."[2]

Neoliberal regulatory structures established in both Canada and Colombia have proven particularly harmful in the oil sector, where the energy security of both countries has been undermined in favour of economic growth and the profits of multinational corporations. And while handing over the national resource wealth to multinational corporations, the Canadian and Colombian governments have overseen a dramatic decline in the quality of health care, education and other social programs. While this is also the neoliberal reality in many other resource-rich nations of the world, some South American countries are challenging the global capitalist model, on both the national and international levels. Venezuela has been at the forefront of this emerging movement, as it challenges neoliberalism by empowering the citizenry and ensuring the country's vast natural resource wealth benefits all Venezuelans. Consequently, it has come to exemplify an alternative for many around the world.

A Venezuelan Alternative: The Bolivarian Revolution

Like many other nations in the global South, Venezuela implemented neoliberal reforms during the 1980s and 1990s, which contributed to a dramatic increase in the country's poverty levels. As occured in Canada, Colombia and many other oil-rich nations, the adoption of neoliberalism in Venezuela gave multinational energy companies access to the country's oil reserves on favourable terms.[3] But by the late 1990s, Venezuela's traditional parties had become thoroughly discredited, along with the neoliberal model they promoted. Venezuelans sought an alternative and, on December 6, 1998, they elected Hugo Chávez to the presidency with 57 per cent of the vote—the largest percentage total in four decades of Venezuelan democracy.[4] On assuming office, Chávez immediately set about fulfilling his campaign promise to establish a new constitution and to ensure that all Venezuelans benefited from the wealth generated by the country's vast oil reserves.

The new Bolivarian Constitution, formulated by an elected constitutional assembly and approved in a national referendum, prohibited the privatization of the Venezuelan state oil company (PDVSA) and endowed all twenty-six million Venezuelans with the right to free health care and education, including post-secondary schooling. And then, in 2001, the Chávez government announced the *Organic Law of Hydrocarbons*, which states that the oil sector must serve the "sustainable development of the country" by using its revenues to finance "health, education, a macro-economic stabilization fund and productive investment ... for the welfare of the people."[5] The law also decreed that PDVSA hold a majority share in all joint ventures with foreign companies. Additionally, it raised the royalty rates that foreign oil companies pay to the Venezuelan government. These increased from 16.6 per cent a barrel to between 20 and 30 per cent for conventional oil and from 1 per cent to 16.6 per cent for heavy crude.[6] In 2006, the latter royalty rate would be further raised to 33.3 per cent, and the income tax rate for oil companies increased to 50 per cent from 34 per cent.[7]

Capitalist elites—both domestic and international—claimed that the new law would deter foreign investment and drive multinational oil companies out of Venezuela. In the ensuing years, however, companies reluctantly began renegotiating their contracts with PDVSA. After eight companies signed new deals in 2005, industry analyst Roger Tissot of PFC Energy in Washington, DC, noted, "This is a victory for the Venezuelan government because these eight companies have agreed to tougher terms. The remaining companies may be trying to negotiate a better deal, but I don't see anyone disputing what appears to be a *fait accompli*, and I certainly don't see a stampede out of Venezuela."[8] There has not been a stampede out of Venezuela because multinational oil companies are still making huge profits, despite the new regulations. While global oil prices were more than $100 a barrel for much of 2008, it only cost oil companies $34 a barrel under the new contract terms to produce heavy crude in Venezuela's Orinoco Basin, and much less for conventional crude.[9]

Unlike in Colombia and Canada, Venezuela's oil policies run contrary to neoliberal doctrine and ensure that the government, and by extension the Venezuelan people, are the primary beneficiaries of the country's oil wealth. While the government's policies have proven popular with the majority of the population, most of whom live in poverty, the country's capitalist elites have vehemently opposed Chávez's rule. In fact, politics in Venezuela under Chávez are constantly referred to as "polarized," only because the hegemonic role of capitalist elites has been challenged. In reality, the country is no more polarized than it was under neoliberalism.[10] The media and mainstream analysts placed little emphasis on polarization until the poor became the benefactors of policy-making. In actuality, the polarization that should have been troubling observers is not the sharply differing political perspectives of the rich and poor in Venezuela, but the country's grossly unequal distribution of wealth—the problem that the Chávez government is attempting to address.

No amount of persuasion is going to convince those who have enjoyed the privilege of controlling Venezuela's oil wealth for decades that they should share this wealth. Capitalist elites are bound to find the process of wealth redistribution painful and to view the policies associated with redistribution as "authoritarian." Interestingly, it is not suggested that this is the bitter medicine that capitalist elites must swallow to achieve a more just and humane society. Whereas the poor, by contrast, had been asked to swallow the bitter medicine of neoliberal austerity for more than two decades in the vain hope that some of the wealth would eventually trickle down.

Rather than continuing to wait and see if national wealth would eventually trickle down to the country's impoverished majority, the Chávez government has instead challenged neoliberal doctrine by using its increased oil revenues to fund social programs to benefit the poor. The Bolivarian revolution, as the Chávez government's reforms are called, is intended to constitute an alternative to the neoliberal model the wealthy nations of the global North imposed on the South. At the United Nations in 2004, Chávez issued one of his many scathing critiques of neoliberalism when he declared, "Hunger and poverty are the most terrible of the effects of a world order based on neoliberal globalization. [...] A world without poor and hungry would be achievable only through an economic and social order radically different from that which now prevails."[11]

For a majority of Venezuelans, the Bolivarian revolution represents that radically different economic and social order as it challenges elite control of the economy and seeks to create a new society in which all citizens are empowered. One strategy the government has used to achieve this goal is educating people about their political, social and economic rights under the new constitution. In Venezuela, the constitution is everywhere. It is a best-selling book. There are cartoon depictions of it in schools. Many food packages in the new state-subsidized markets are adorned with a specific article of the constitution and a cartoon illustrating the significance of that article. A package of sugar, for example, quotes article 103, which states that all people have the right to a good quality education for free. Above the text is a cartoon illustration of independence hero Simón Bolívar taking his two children to school. Other food packages contain articles of the constitution concerning the right to food, as well as the right to be free from police brutality and government corruption.

In Barrio 23 de Enero (23rd of January), one of the largest poor neighbourhoods in Caracas, the government's local representative, Lisandro Pérez, claims that the Bolivarian revolution seeks to empower citizens so that they will become passionate about social change. This change, says Pérez, cannot come from above; it must be rooted in local communities. The objective is to create a new socialism that is different from the rigid centralized socialism of the 20th century. As Pérez explains, "When the Berlin Wall fell, we thought it was the fall of socialism, but that wasn't true. What was the significance of the fall of the Berlin Wall? In reality, it was the fall of the old models, the old orthodoxy, and something new was rising. [...] It had to fall so that a new political project could rise, like President Chávez's, which is now underway."[12]

In other words, the central government cannot be allowed to strictly dictate and control the new socialist project, as so often occurred during the 20th century. Instead, the role of the national government is to facilitate and provide logistical support for community-based initiatives. As Pérez points out, the desire to implement radical change long preceded Chávez's election, "But now we have a government that helps facilitate revolutionary projects at the community level instead of using repression to crush them."[13]

The Venezuelan project represents a process of repoliticization from the community to the national level, which is why Chávez is seen as such a threat by capitalist elites, both within and outside of Venezuela. An important component of the Chávez government's revolution has been to address the country's health care crisis. Beyond the delivery of services, health care is seen as an arena for active citizenship. In fact, it is framed in the constitution as both a right and a responsibility. The rights component deals with questions of accessibility, while the responsibility component involves emphasis both on preventive health strategies and citizens' participation in the design and support of community level health care initiatives.

Before Chávez's election victory, Venezuela's public health system was seriously underfunded and not readily accessible to poor Venezuelans living in urban shantytowns and rural areas. For many poor Venezuelans, visiting a doctor meant travelling long distances, followed by hours waiting in line. According to minister of health and social development Francisco Armada:

> We practiced neoliberal politics during the last two decades of the last century, similar to what was happening in the rest of Latin America. This was setting us up legally for a private healthcare system a lot like the Chilean model, although not exactly.[14]

While privatization did not pose a problem for the country's middle and upper classes, who were already paying for high-quality private health care, it threatened to make access to health care for the poor even more difficult. To redress the inequitable access to health care and reverse the privatization process, article 83 of the Bolivarian constitution enshrined the right to free universal and equitable health care. Armada explained, "As a country, we decided that health was a fundamental and prioritized human and social right, including being above other rights. For example, being above commercial rights."[15]

In a trade deal that challenges the free trade mantra of neoliberalism, Venezuela exchanges ninety thousand barrels of oil a day for twenty thousand Cuban doctors, medical technicians, physical fitness trainers and literacy experts.[16] In other words, instead of engaging in the capitalist concept of an international trading system in which the principal actors are private corporations whose primary objective is making a profit, Venezuela and Cuba are participating in a society-to-society barter process ensuring that one country will have the doctors it desperately needs while the other obtains the energy supplies it frequently lacks.

The Cuban doctors work in poor Venezuelan neighbourhoods under Misión Barrio Adentro (Into the Neighbourhood Mission), initiated in 2003 in the impoverished municipality of Libertador, located on the steep hillsides surrounding the capital, Caracas. Armada described the project:

> We had difficulty getting Venezuelan doctors to participate in this process, so we began working with Cuban doctors. The community itself established the places where the doctors would be located; many families contributed parts of their own homes. The community assumed the responsibility for the security of the doctors, sharing their food and many other aspects of the process. And it is this process, this combination of forces that we want to highlight, because in it we see the recipe for success with an organized community that not only makes demands, but also participates in its right to health.[17]

The goal of Barrio Adentro is to make good quality health care available to all Venezuelans, particularly the marginalized poor. By the end of 2004, Venezuela had close to nine thousand new primary care clinics.[18] In its first eighteen months, the program made services available to seventeen million previously marginalized Venezuelans and the director of the Pan American Health Organization praised Chávez for his leadership in health.[19]

By 2005 in Barrio 23 de Enero, the government had used oil revenues to fund more than ninety primary care clinics to serve the community's 300,000 residents, many of whom live in small brick houses stacked precariously one above the other on steep hillsides overlooking the city centre. The Cuban doctors hold office hours from eight in the morning until noon and perform house calls during the afternoons. They live in the sector where they work and are on call twenty-four hours a day. According to a female patient waiting to see a Cuban doctor in one of the new clinics, "The programme has been good for the community. There were no doctors in 23 de Enero before Barrio Adentro."[20] Meanwhile, the physical fitness trainers are responsible for educating citizens about general health issues and how to care for their bodies. The trainers routinely hold exercise classes and, along with the doctors, meet regularly with health committees comprising local residents to discuss community health needs. Tibisay Miranda, a resident of the La Cañada section of Barrio 23 de Enero, claims that "people in the community who barely knew their neighbours before are now organizing themselves."[21]

The neighbourhood health committees represent an important element of the government's approach to health care: citizens, particularly poor citizens, should not be seen merely as passive recipients of health care policy. The process of achieving the program's goals in health care requires the active participation of communities in examining the health of neighbourhoods, as part of a larger project of social transformation. Communities achieve this transformation through local government, various types of neighbourhood associations and health and school committees. These groups are responsible for identifying their community's needs and for contributing to the design and continuing evaluation of programs to solve local problems. In this sense, community members need to take responsibility for leadership in health and education so that they themselves will be accountable.[22] The government, says health minister Armada, does not believe in prepackaged programs, and projects such as Barrio Adentro require active citizen participation to work.[23]

The government links its approach to education intrinsically to its health care philosophy: that a vibrant democracy requires the active participation of citizens who are well-nourished, healthy and educated. Under neoliberalism, the underfunded public education system, like many in Latin America, was deteriorating, while enrolment in private schools increased steadily. Many poor families could not afford to send their children to school, and so thousands were excluded from the system. In 1998, average enrolment consisted of only 59 per cent of children and, as a result, more than 1.5 million Venezuelans were illiterate. Furthermore, more than 2 million students had dropped out before grade six and another two million had failed to complete their secondary education.[24]

To address this crisis, the Chávez administration is transforming the country's primary and secondary schools from traditional institutions to Bolivarian schools. The Bolivarian schools contain kitchens staffed with parents from the community who have completed an intensive state-funded nutrition course. The school kitchens provide students with breakfast, lunch and an afternoon snack in an attempt to lower the levels of malnutrition among poor Venezuelan children. The Bolivarian schools also contain computer labs so that all Venezuelan children, and not only those from wealthy families, have the opportunity to become computer literate, as they should be in the 21st century. By 2005, more than 3,500 schools had benefited from the transformation process and more than a million previously excluded children were receiving free education and meals.[25] In Barrio 23 de Enero, twelve of the neighbourhood's twenty-two schools had been transformed to the Bolivarian model by 2005. According to Arnaldo Sotillo, director of one of the Bolivarian schools in the barrio, the overall objective of the new schools is to emphasize "social values and create a different citizen for the future, a better society overall. The only way to change society is through education."[26]

The Chávez government has also established agricultural and manufacturing co-operatives throughout the country, which in some ways reflect the Antigonish Movement's "middle way" between laissez-faire capitalism and state socialism. In 2003, the state oil company turned an unused storage facility in Caracas into a community complex called Fabricio Ojeda, which now contains three co-operatives producing textiles, footwear and agriculture. The Fabricio Ojeda complex also houses a popular clinic, popular pharmacy, food market, agricultural plots, various exercise facilities and an office selling discounted urban transportation tickets to students. PDVSA provided loans to the textile co-operative established by 280 women from the local community. The women used the PDVSA funding to construct a building, using local labour, and to purchase the necessary machinery and materials to begin producing military and school uniforms, clothing, bags and other textile products. The co-operative is providing inexpensive uniforms to schools and the military, and selling its other products to stores and vendors around Caracas. By participating in the co-operative, previously marginalized women have achieved a sense of empowerment. As co-operative member Louisa Ruiz declared, "We are no longer staying in the house; we are business women now."[27]

The Bolivarian revolution has not been a strictly nationalist project; Chávez has also placed great emphasis on challenging the international capitalist institutions. He has done this by focusing on regional integration, proposing the Bolivarian Alternative for Latin America and the Caribbean (ALBA) as an alternative to the U.S.-pushed free trade model. Free trade agreements require that nations in Latin America and throughout the global South, regardless of their level of development, compete economically with the United States and others in the North in a "free" market. ALBA, by contrast, calls for solidarity with those countries with the weakest economies through the creation of a "Compensatory Fund for Structural Convergence." The fund is intended to facilitate a transfer of resources from the better performing economies to the weaker ones, similar to the transfer system used by member nations of the European Union. The Bolivarian regional alternative also advocates agricultural policies to contribute to food self-sufficiency among member nations, rather than the export-oriented neoliberal agricultural model.[28]

Chávez has shown that his desire to help the region reduce its dependency on U.S.-dominated international financial institutions such as the IMF and World Bank is more than mere rhetoric. In July 2005, Venezuela loaned $300 million to Ecuador so that that country could avoid defaulting on its foreign debt. Venezuela issued the loan after the World Bank refused to disburse a previously agreed-to $100 million loan because the IMF was not satisfied with the pace of Ecuador's neoliberal reforms.[29] In May 2007, after finally paying off the last of the pre-Chávez-era loans, the Venezuelan president announced that the country was quitting the IMF and the World Bank.[30] And then, six months later, Venezuela and six other South American nations—Argentina, Brazil, Bolivia, Ecuador, Paraguay and Uruguay—announced their intention to create the Bank of the South. The new bank, unlike the IMF and World Bank, will provide unconditional loans for development projects to liberate governments in the South from the need to implement neoliberal reforms.[31] In June 2008, ministers from the seven nations agreed to provide the bank with $10 billion in initial funding.[32]

Meanwhile, in June 2005, to achieve a regional redistribution of Venezuela's oil wealth, Chávez launched the Petrocaribe initiative, ensuring delivery of affordable oil to thirteen poor Caribbean nations. According to Chávez, resource-rich nations like Venezuela that are reaping the benefits of high oil prices have a responsibility to help their less fortunate neighbours, whose people are suffering as a result of high fuel costs. Venezuela was already supplying subsidized oil to several Caribbean nations, but under Petrocaribe, Caracas agreed to absorb 40 per cent of the cost of oil supplies whenever the price surpasses $50 a barrel.[33]

In contrast to the externally oriented neoliberal development model, Venezuela's Bolivarian revolution promotes a nationally rooted but regionally integrated approach to development and poverty issues where economic growth alone does not determine development possibilities. The dramatic transformations taking place in health and education in Venezuela are indicative of what can happen when poor communities begin to participate in decision-making. A majority of Venezuelans have made clear that the prepackaged neoliberal agenda does not serve their needs and that the government's efforts to respond to this citizen input has forced a confrontation with capitalist elites—both at home and abroad. However, the qualitative improvements in democratic participation in Venezuela have not required the overrepresentation of capitalist elites—in fact, democracy is working quite well without them playing a dominant role.

Venezuela's Bolivarian revolution clearly illustrates that implementing neoliberalism—particularly in nations of the North such as Canada—is an ideologically motivated, conscious policy decision. The Chávez government has shown that there are alternative policy directions that can help facilitate participatory democracy, community-based initiatives, and regional cooperation on a level rarely, if ever, seen under capitalism. Athough many social problems persist in Venezuela, such as high crime rates, that the Chávez government has so far failed to effectively address, our intention here has been to highlight those aspects of the Bolivarian revolution that provide positive examples of alternative policies. Perhaps the most stunning shift in social indicators is that the Chávez government's policies resulted in the percentage of Venezuelans living in poverty being reduced from 50 per cent when Chávez assumed office in 1999 to 33 percent by 2007.[34]

The Bolivarian revolution is in many ways a positive example for nations in both the North and South, but there is one problem that is impossible to overlook; in fact, it represents a fundamental flaw in the model. Despite the challenges it poses to neoliberalism, the Bolivarian revolution remains reliant on fossil fuel production and the global capitalist oil market. While it is understandable that the Chávez government would want to exploit Venezuela's vast oil reserves in order to address the country's dire social crisis, the reliance on fossil fuels and the global capitalist market means that the revolution in its present form is unsustainable environmentally. In some ways, the Venezuelan alternative seeks to replace industrial capitalism with industrial socialism—albeit a far more democratic industrial socialism than existed in 20th-century models. However, while industrial socialism may successfully address many of the social inequities inherent in the capitalist system, ultimately it is no more sustainable from an environmental perspective.

The Environmental Challenge

Capitalist elites have responded to the growing evidence of global warming and other serious environmental concerns by posing market solutions as a means of solving problems inherent in the capitalist system. In a strategy to boost their image and defer binding governmental regulations, corporations have initiated social and environmental responsibility programs. These programs suggest that redirecting a small percentage of their earnings toward community projects and environmental initiatives will solve the social and environmental problems caused by their profit-taking activities. However, such efforts are tantamount to placing a band-aid on a severed appendage, and they do little to address the root cause of the problem: the growth imperative inherent in capitalism. As Indian philosopher and physicist Vandana Shiva points out:

> Economic growth takes place through the exploitation of natural resources. Deforestation creates growth. Mining of groundwater creates growth. Overfishing creates growth. Further economic growth cannot help regenerate the very spheres which must be destroyed for economic growth to occur. Nature shrinks as capital grows. The growth of the market cannot solve the very crisis it creates.[35]

Nevertheless, political representatives—or "green" diplomats—representing the interests of capitalist elites, promote international environmental agreements that give the illusion of addressing the problem when, in reality, their goals inevitably fall far short of those required to solve the ecological crisis. Meanwhile, other capitalists claim that the innovative nature of capitalism and its corresponding technological advances will ultimately address all environmental problems. However, history suggests otherwise. In fact, despite the impressive technological advances of the past half-century, the degree of environmental damage—particularly related to global warming—has not decreased, but increased during this period. As political scientist Lee-Anne Broadhead points out:

> The heartfelt efforts of green diplomats to bridge the gap between economics and environmental issues is doomed to fail because of their acceptance of the destructive practices inherent in the growth ethic. Economic growth and the organization of international society around the goals of efficient capital mobility and the profit margin its controllers seek are inherently anti-ecological. Any way it is looked at, the extraction of raw materials for the manufacture of goods—the demand for which in many cases has been artificially created—does not lead to an ecologically sound existence. No amount of masking the reality with talk of environmentally friendly technologies will offset the destructiveness of the growth ethic when the resounding failure of the technological fix is taken into consideration.[36]

Some political leaders, such as U.S. president George W. Bush and Canadian prime minister Stephen Harper, have unabashedly refused to legislate cuts to greenhouse gas emissions under the Kyoto Protocol because of the potential economic repercussions. Their attitudes are emblematic of the collective denial of reality occurring in both the North and South with regard to the sustainability of capitalism. The only explanation for such a state of denial is a blind faith in the ability of the capitalist system to maintain itself and to miraculously solve the problems of gross social inequality and looming environmental catastrophe.

This collective denial of reality allows leaders such as Bush and Harper to convince people that the modern materialistic lifestyle can be maintained indefinitely, thereby permitting citizens to continue their daily consumer practices. In fact, Bush has urged the American people to increase their consumption on several occasions. In December 2006, the U.S. president announced that it was important to keep the country's economy growing, saying "I encourage you all to go shopping more."[37] In February 2008, Bush stated, "Consumerism is a significant part of our GDP growth, and we want to sustain the American consumer, encourage the American consumer and, at the same time, we want to encourage investment."[38]

Any shift away from the unsustainable capitalist model to an environmentally sustainable society would undoubtedly require a dramatic reduction in levels of consumption and a serious re-evaluation of priorities, on both the individual and community levels. But achieving such a shift is clearly an uphill battle because, as Broadhead notes, "Those intent on raising awareness of environmental issues in the overdeveloped countries face a public addicted to commodity consumption and fearful of the language of limits."[39]

Regardless of the rhetoric of capitalist elites, the fact that there are ecological "limits" is an inescapable reality. As noted earlier, the capitalist system is predicated on the impoverishment of a significant portion of the global population, to ensure a steady supply of cheap labour and natural resources. It is also predicated on the impoverishment of nature and the environment. The capitalist development model being promoted throughout the global South is impossible to achieve, because the planet's ecosystem cannot sustain six-and-a-half billion people living the same lifestyle currently enjoyed by the majority of people in the global North. For instance, with only 4 per cent of the world's population, the U.S. consumes 25 per cent of global energy production. Additionally, the United States consumes 50 per cent of the global production of raw materials and generates 40 per cent of the world's waste.[40] It does not take a scientific or mathematical genius to figure out that there are not enough raw materials and energy to go around, or enough space on the planet to deposit the waste, to allow three or four billion more people in the global South to achieve the same lifestyle.

China's economic boom is a clear illustration that the capitalist development model is not viable for the majority of people in the South. China's integration into the global capitalist economy during the past twenty years, and its consequent economic growth, has resulted in the country experiencing high levels of inequality similar to those of most other countries under neoliberalism. The economic boom has created a new urban middle class of 150-200 million people—a number that is expected to double over the next five years—who are now enjoying lifestyles comparable to those of many people in the global North.[41] Meanwhile, the country's poorest province, Guizhou, has a GDP per capita lower than Bangladesh, Senegal and Uganda.[42]

China's economic growth and the corresponding elevation of almost 200 million people to middle-class status through capitalist development is already raising alarm bells about natural resources and global warming. The new middle class in China constitutes only 20 per cent of that country's total population and a mere 6 per cent of the 3.3 billion people in the South who currently live in poverty. Given the burden placed on both the earth's resources and the environment that has resulted from elevating a mere 6 per cent of the world's impoverished population to a lifestyle equivalent to that enjoyed in the North, it is inconceivable that the promise of capitalist development can be fulfilled for everyone on the planet.

Like the global capitalist powers before it, China has followed the traditional fossil-fuel based, capitalist development path and, as a result, it now generates 80 per cent of its electricity with coal.[43] Furthermore, the Chinese government plans to build more than four hundred new coal-fired power plants over the next 20 years.[44] The Asian giant is not relying solely on coal to fuel its development; it is also scouring the world for increasingly scarce supplies of oil. In 2003, China surpassed Japan to become the world's second largest consumer of oil—after the United States—and its rapidly growing consumption is a major contributor to high oil prices.[45]

Some energy experts have estimated that global oil production may peak in the next five years.[46] Thereafter, as global demand continues to increase, global production will steadily decline. The fact that "Peak Oil" is rapidly approaching and that the era of cheap oil is over has been made apparent by our growing need to exploit increasingly expensive and difficult-to-access reserves, such as Alberta's oil sands and Venezuela's heavy crude in the Orinoco Basin. And yet, capitalist production and consumption habits continue to rely on oil.

Neoliberal capitalism is premised on the doctrine of economic growth and free trade. To continually achieve growth, corporations must keep producing and selling products. A significant percentage of the goods produced in the world today are made, at least in part, with plastic, a by-product of petroleum. Therefore, the manufacture of most of the clothes, shoes, televisions, computers, cell phones, household appliances, cars, electronic gadgets, CDs, DVDs, pesticides and literally millions of other things we take for granted in our daily lives rely on oil. Global capitalism also requires a huge supply of oil to transport these goods from their production sites to markets located in every corner of the world. Most of the goods produced by the global capitalist system are transported by oil-guzzling trucks and ships, with the volume of global container shipping tripling over the past fifteen years.[47] In short, the global capitalist system depends on the perpetual production of petroleum-based goods and the perpetual consumption of these products—many of which are luxury items manufactured for the amusement of consumers in the North. Consequently, it is difficult to accept that the capitalist model is even sustainable for people in the North, never mind the entire global population. Clearly, a sustainable society cannot be dependent on a global trading system and fossil fuels. Rather, it must be based, to the greatest degree possible, on self-sufficiency, social and economic equality, and environmental sustainability.

Under neoliberalism, it is impossible to establish a mostly self-sufficient, sustainable and egalitarian model at the local level because the objective of existing regulatory and legal frameworks at the provincial, national and international levels is to serve the interests of capitalist elites. For example, communities in Cape Breton cannot ban the use of coal for electricity generation and replace it with a cheaper, clean, renewable energy source such as wind because utilities fall under provincial jurisdiction. The pro-neoliberal attitudes of the Nova Scotia provincial government not only led it to privatize Nova Scotia Power but also to provide the utility company with a virtual monopoly over the distribution of electrical power. Under existing provincial regulations, only a utility company can transmit electricity across property lines. Consequently, members of a Cape Breton community such as Main-à-Dieu, Louisbourg or Cheticamp cannot work cooperatively to erect a wind turbine to generate electricity for its residents, as has been done in many European communities. Such an endeavour to generate environmentally friendly energy at the local level in Nova Scotia would violate provincial regulations because the electricity would have to be transmitted across property lines. And even if the regulations were modified to allow cooperatively owned electricity generation systems, Cape Bretoners would still be forced to endure the pollution emitted by NSP's three coal-fired power plants on the island which would continue generating electricity for mainland Nova Scotia. Consequently, the only solution to the ecological devastation caused by fossil fuels is to achieve structural change at the local, national and international levels.

Despite the prevailing hegemonic power of neoliberal capitalism, several examples of relatively self-sufficient and sustainable communities exist around the world. Some are indigenous communities that have managed to maintain their traditional cultures and lifestyles in the face of the onslaught of globalization. Others are modern attempts to establish a sustainable model on the local level. These communities provide invaluable insights into how a post-capitalist society might function. One such example is the community of Las Gaviotas in rural Colombia.

A Colombian Alternative: Las Gaviotas

In the early 1970s, Paolo Lugari set out to build a sustainable community in the inhospitable and extremely remote environs of the Department of Vichada in Los Llanos—the plains—in eastern Colombia. More than thirty years later, the community of Las Gaviotas is recognized by the United Nations Development Programme (UNDP) and held up as an example by many advocates of sustainable living around the world.

Lugari chose a 28,000-hectare area in Los Llanos specifically because of its harsh climate and geographic remoteness. A scorching tropical sun and temperatures that reach as high as 40 degrees Celsius mark the five-month dry season. The remaining seven months of the year consist of torrential tropical rains that render most of the roads in Los Llanos impassable. There are few trees in the region, and some of the worst soils in Colombia. Furthermore, Las Gaviotas has had to survive in the midst of Colombia's ongoing civil conflict, which has made the community inaccessible to most outsiders. As Lugari, the son of an Italian geography professor, explains, "We always put social experiments in the easiest, most fertile places. We wanted the hardest place. If we could do it there, we could do it anywhere."[48]

The two hundred residents of Las Gaviotas enjoy free food, lodging, health care and schooling, while earning more than double the Colombian minimum wage. The community maintains an egalitarian social structure in which everyone participates in community decision-making and no one is in a position of authority. Also, the community has no poverty, no police, no jail and no crime. While residents have come and gone over the years, the overall population of the community has increased steadily during the past two decades. According to Richard White and Gloria Gonzalez, authors of "Las Gaviotas: Sustainability in the Tropics":

> Over the years, some 30 children have been born in the village and some 500 children from the village and from the surrounding region have attended the Gaviotas school. Adult residents rotate among the various jobs in the village, from construction to planting to gardening to cooking. Among other benefits, this equips everyone to contribute creatively to improving productivity and to overall satisfaction. Four residents are on pension after working for 25 years.[49]

Despite the back-to-earth and seemingly commune-like nature of Las Gaviotas, journalist Alan Weisman points out that the community's residents

> aren't free love hippies, they're serious people committed to flourishing in a world of shrinking resources. After nearly a quarter century, Gaviotas makes already stale phrases like sustainable development and appropriate technology seem not just believable, but fresh and surprising.[50]

When Lugari and a diverse group of collaborators that included artists, engineers and local indigenous people founded Las Gaviotas, they decided to develop original technologies suited to the tropics, rather than rely on technology from the North. As Lugari explains, "When we import solutions from the U.S. or Europe, we also import their problems."[51] The litany of environmentally friendly, technological innovations developed in Las Gaviotas are impressive: compact windmills that weigh less than one hundred pounds and yet generate electricity from both soft tropical breezes and the strong wind gusts accompanying thunderstorms during the rainy season; unique manual water pumps reaching a greater depth than conventional ones, thereby allowing access to low-lying water tables

during the dry season; a special see-saw in the playground that ac-
tivates one of the water pumps when the children play on it; solar
water heating systems; a solar water distiller provides pure water for
medical emergencies; a hydroponic farm for cultivating vegetables
and fruits; solar-powered hot-oil pressure cookers; and stovetop
burners fuelled with methane gas generated from cow manure.[52]

Las Gaviotas has exported its innovative technology to other
parts of Colombia. Solar water heating systems designed in Las
Gaviotas now heat Colombia's presidential palace, three huge apart-
ment complexes—one consisting of 7,500 units—in the cities of
Bogotá and Medellín, and one of the country's largest hospitals.
The solar water systems are virtually maintenance free because they
contain no moving parts. Additionally, numerous rural agricultural
communities in Colombia are benefiting from windmills and water
pumps designed in Las Gaviotas.[53]

One of the more ingenious inventions in Las Gaviotas was the
community's self-sufficient rural hospital facility. On a visit to Las
Gavoitas in the mid-1990s, journalist Weisman described the hospital as

> an extraordinary building set on a rise, a maze of angles formed
> by skylights, glass awnings, solar collectors, and brushed steel col-
> umns. The *Japanese Architectural Journal* has named this, the 16-
> bed Gaviotas hospital, one of the 40 most important buildings in
> the world.[54]

White and Gonzalez describe the inner workings of the medical facility:

> Despite external temperatures that can exceed 38 degrees Celsius,
> with very high humidity, the one-of-a-kind facility provided ap-
> propriate climate control for an operating room, using bio-climat-
> ic technologies such as sub-surface tunnels and double ventilation
> systems on the walls and roof. The kitchen featured solar cooking,
> although repeated efforts to design an effective solar refrigerator
> never succeeded. Patient rooms included louvered windows for
> ventilation and sliding roof panels that would admit daylight and
> allow for disinfection by exposure to ultraviolet sunlight. The hos-
> pital was enhanced by a *maloca*, a tall open-sided thatch-roofed
> structure built by indigenous Guahibo neighbors to provide shel-
> ter for families of patients staying close to loved ones.[55]

The largest project at Las Gaviotas has been a massive reforestation project intended to improve soil quality so the community is not solely reliant on hydroponic farming. Thousands of years ago Los Llanos was part of the Amazon rainforest, the northern edge of which now lies several hundred miles to the south of Las Gaviotas. Lugari and his colleagues discovered that the Caribbean Pine would grow in the poor quality acidic soil of Los Llanos and so they set about returning part of the mostly barren plains to their former rainforest glory. The pine plantings represented the beginning of one of the most impressive reforestation projects on the planet. As the pine trees grew, the increasing shade led to lower soil temperatures and higher levels of moisture retention. Other plants soon began to grow in the cool moist soil beneath the palms and, instead of removing them as is common practice on monoculture plantations, the Las Gaviotas team allowed them to sprout. An increasing number and variety of plants emerged, contributing to improved soil quality. The biodiversity of the emerging forest has proven to be astounding with more than 190 different plant species established or re-established to date. Additionally, the abundance of flora has attracted increasing numbers of animals, contributing to the creation of an entire rainforest ecosystem covering eight thousand hectares. Meanwhile, because the Caribbean Pines are sterile in Los Llanos, they will eventually die off and leave behind a naturally regenerated rainforest providing carbon sequestration to help combat global warming.[56]

While the geographic remoteness of Las Gaviotas has protected it to some degree from the global capitalist economic system, the community has still been forced to contend with the threat posed by neoliberal globalization. One of the casualties has been the hospital, which was ordered closed by the Colombian government because it violated the country's new health care regulations. The violations had nothing to do with health and safety; rather they contravened the new guidelines for private health care established as part of the country's neoliberal reforms. Ironically, despite its communal nature, the Gaviotas hospital fell under the category of a private health care facility because it was not a State-run medical centre. The new regulations, modelled on the U.S. private managed-care system, require private hospitals to have at least three doctors, which the sparsely populated region of Los Llanos could not support. Also, Las Gaviotas and the surrounding region could not meet the minimum subscriber base required for private health care facilities. Undeterred, the people of Las Gaviotas again turned an apparent negative into a positive by taking advantage of the fact that the hospital was a sterile facility and transforming it into a centre for producing potable water. The pure water is distributed to local residents for free and has dramatically lowered the previously high rates of gastrointestinal disease.[57]

Las Gaviotas has also been affected in other ways by the implementation of neoliberalism in Colombia. The dismantling of Keynesian-inspired protectionist policies in the 1990s led to a dramatic increase in imports, particularly foodstuffs. The cheap imported food products hurt many of Colombia's small farmers and by extension Las Gaviotas, which had generated some of its revenues from selling its electricity-generating windmills and manual water pumps to agricultural communities throughout Colombia.

Las Gaviotas has also sought to challenge neoliberalism. For example, the community has generated revenues through the sale of its innovations, but does not receive nearly as much as it could because it does not patent its inventions, preferring instead to share the technology for free. This policy has not only challenged neoliberal doctrine on intellectual property rights, it has also led to Las Gaviotas having an influence far beyond Colombia's borders, as communities throughout Latin America have copied the designs of its windmill, water pump and other devices.

While Las Gaviotas is representative of the challenges of establishing local alternatives within a broader capitalist context, its achievements nevertheless stand as a powerful illustration of how a mostly self-sufficient, egalitarian, sustainable, post-capitalist society could function. Las Gaviotas lacks many of the material luxuries that most people living in industrial capitalist societies expect and demand, but its residents believe they have achieved a more sustainable happiness. As one resident points out, "We believe austerity is a better path to happiness than too much comfort. In Colombia's oil camps, what have they gotten? Prostitution and alcoholism, because salaries are too high. Then the oil is gone. What's left is misery. Meanwhile, we plant trees, so the atmosphere won't disappear."[58]

Gibbs and Leech

Local and Global Linkages

The practical example of Las Gaviotas suggests that a mostly self-sufficient, sustainable and egalitarian model on the local level is possible. While Las Gaviotas is a small rural community in a world of ever-expanding megacities, we believe it still provides a valuable starting point for seeking local solutions in both rural and urban settings. Meanwhile, Venezuela's Bolivarian revolution illustrates just how viable such local alternatives can be when the State prioritizes such development projects over serving the interests of capitalist elites. Perhaps most importantly, these examples illustrate how much we in the global North can learn from peoples in the global South. There are already commonalities between emerging local alternatives in Cape Breton and those in the global South. For example, a campaign is under way in Cape Breton to change the provincial regulations prohibiting communities from co-operatively generating electricity with wind turbines as residents in Las Gaviotas are already doing. Cape Bretoners are also trying to establish a Local Employment Trading System, which could be considered a community-level version of the oil-for-doctors barter agreement between Venezuela and Cuba. Some residents of Cape Breton are also working to establish a green transportation network and a more people-friendly urban environment. However, such local efforts to challenge the corporate-dominated neoliberal model often fall far short of their full potential in the face of the ideologically opposed policies implemented at the municipal, provincial, national and international levels of governance. Consequently, it is essential that local communities, not only in Cape Breton, but also throughout Canada and the rest of the world, make efforts to create change in solidarity with other communities, if they are to successfully challenge the neoliberal structures currently obstructing them.

Many ideological and practical alternatives are emerging around the world, advocating such a global resistance to neoliberalism. The International Forum on Globalization (IFG) and Vandana Shiva's "earth democracy" are but two examples. Shiva calls for a reclaiming of the global commons in the interests of social justice, sustainability and cultural integrity.[59] The IFG, which represents a diverse global community, promotes a variety of initiatives "linked together in common rejection of the illegitimate power and false promises of global corporations and a proactive commitment to revitalize democracy at local, regional, national and global levels. Each contributes to an emerging vision of the healthy, just and sustainable society that humanity has the means to create."[60]

The ever-growing alternative globalization movement currently comprises millions of people, from Cape Breton to Colombia and beyond. According to Broadhead, the movement is integrated

> ...in the sense that most people, in most parts of the world, can be appealed to on the grounds that they are in some way or other a victim of the corporate greed, government complacency, or environmental destruction that are by-products of the neoliberal system. There are no generational, gender, or location differences here. There are different struggles with different objectives, but all together they form a chorus demanding a voice, and that voice will be difficult to suppress.[61]

At its core, that voice is demanding social justice on a global scale through the replacement of an unsustainable, fossil fuel-based capitalist economic model with a more democratic, egalitarian and sustainable alternative.

Conclusion

We Have Met the Enemy

More than three hundred years of capitalism has not only resulted in gross social inequalities globally, it has also devastated the environment, thereby threatening the existence of everyone, the haves and the have-nots. The challenge of eliminating global capitalism and replacing it with a more democratic, egalitarian and sustainable model may seem unrealistic, if not impossible, to most people. However, we have no choice. After more than three centuries of capitalism as the dominant economic model, more than half of the world's population lives in poverty and millions more struggle daily just to keep their heads above the poverty line. Meanwhile, in a world with so much wealth, UNICEF reports that more than one million children under the age of five die each year in the global South because they lack access to safe drinking water and adequate sanitation.[1]

At the close of the 20th Century, the UNDP highlighted several global inequalities in a way that illustrates the priorities of the global capitalist system. For instance, an additional $6 billion a year would have ensured that all children in the global South received a basic education; meanwhile, $8 billion was being spent annually on cosmetics in the United States. Similarly, Europeans spent $11 billion a year on ice cream, $2 billion more than it would have cost to provide safe drinking water and adequate sanitation for everyone in the South. And the $17 billion that Americans and Europeans spent annually on pet food would easily have provided basic health care for everyone in the South.[2] Such a degree of global inequality is not simply an unintended consequence of capitalism; it is an essential component of the global capitalist system.

Capitalist elites claim that the worldwide establishment of neoliberalism will ultimately bring the relatively luxurious lifestyle enjoyed by most in the North to everyone on the planet. In other words, it is suggested that by our continually achieving economic growth, all children will not only have access to a basic education, but also be able to beautify themselves to the same degree as people in the United States. Also, everyone in the South will not only have safe drinking water and adequate sanitation, they will also be able to indulge in ice cream on a scale equal to that of Europeans. And in addition to having basic health care, people in the South will be able to spoil their household pets in the same manner as Americans and Europeans.

There is, however, an inherent contradiction in this promise, given that the materialistic, consumer lifestyle prevalent in the North depends on the exploitation and impoverishment of a significant percentage of the world's population. After all, in order for more than six billion people worldwide to enjoy an equally materialistic lifestyle, the majority of the population in the South would have to see a significant increase in their incomes. Any such drastic rise in their incomes would increase the cost of living in the North as a result of higher manufacturing costs for goods produced in the South, thereby diminishing standards of living in wealthy nations. In other words, the majority of people in the South could only achieve a standard of living equal to people in the North if the latter accepted a dramatic decline in their levels of material comfort and the two worlds met somewhere in the middle.

Capitalist elites, however, have worked hard against a convergence of the two worlds with regard to standards of living. Throughout the history of capitalism, they have relied on colonial and neo-colonial structures to ensure access to cheap resources and labour in the global South. For several decades in the 20th Century, the Keynesian policy framework limited the extent to which they could exploit workers in the North and, to a lesser degree, in the South. Consequently, these elites sought to dismantle the Keynesian model and replace it with neoliberalism as soon as the historic moment permitted such a shift. Under the new post-industrial economy in the North, the exploitation of workers has increased. However, it has been in the new economies in the South that capitalist elites have dramatically escalated their exploitation of workers—replicating the labour situation of a century earlier in industrial regions of the North such as Cape Breton.

The profit imperative inherent in capitalism requires the establishment of political and economic structures favourable to wealth accumulation. In other words, capitalist elites, as we have seen in the cases of Cape Breton and Colombia, will always work to ensure that the wages of workers remain depressed while profits continually rise. Or, as Karl Marx stated, capitalism

> establishes an accumulation of misery, corresponding with accumulation of capital. Accumulation of wealth at one pole is, therefore, at the same time accumulation of misery, agony of toil slavery, ignorance, brutality, mental degradation, at the opposite pole.[3]

The increased exploitation of natural resources and labour in the global South under neoliberalism has ensured greater profits for economic elites worldwide and a steady flow of inexpensive consumer products to everyone in the North. The relatively comfortable materialistic lifestyles enjoyed by most in the North—even in economically depressed regions such as Cape Breton—can only be maintained through neocolonial practices that ensure continued access to cheap resources and labour in the South. Consequently, the maintenance of social inequality is an essential component of global capitalism.

Another fundamental flaw in the global capitalist system has been its reliance from its inception on fossil fuels, particularly coal and oil, and we are just now beginning to come to terms with the dire ecological consequences of this reality. But instead of effectively addressing this environmental crisis, capitalist elites have instead promoted neoliberalism, which has only served to intensify our dependence on fossil fuels. Capitalist development has led to dramatically higher levels of fossil fuel use in rapidly industrializing nations such as China and India. As a result, the threat of global warming illustrates that the neoliberal promise—claiming economic growth will raise the standard of living for all peoples to levels enjoyed in the North—is constrained not only by the model's reliance on social inequality, but also by the planet's ecological limitations.

Despite all the socio-economic and environmental evidence illustrating the failure and unsustainability of the global capitalist model, peripheral regions in the North, such as Cape Breton, and peripheral nations in the South, such as Colombia, continue their efforts to integrate themselves into a system that has little use for them beyond the exploitation of their people and natural resources. Cape Breton has spent the past one hundred years trying to move closer to the centre of the capitalist system, yet it remains firmly on the outside looking in. The same scenario applies to Colombia's "development" efforts over the past century. This reality begs the question: Why do Cape Breton, Colombia and other peripheral regions continue to play the capitalist game when they could instead move toward a sustainable and more equitable social and economic model?

As we noted in the case of Colombia, the over-representation of pro-neoliberal elites in the political structures of the state ensures the continuation of the model in that country. Furthermore, international financial institutions and the promise of U.S. military aid ensure that those elites do not deviate from the desired "development" model. The over-representation of pro-neoliberal elites in government also applies to Canada and other wealthy nations, but to what degree is the populace an accomplice to the growth of the unsustainable capitalist model in the global North?

Cartoonist Walt Kelly first used the phrase "We have Met the Enemy and He is Us" on a poster for Earth Day in 1970 to critique the excesses of the capitalist consumer society. His words have a particularly poignant ring in the early 21st century as we face the unprecedented threat of global warming. While many claim that radical alternatives are "unrealistic" in the current context, it has become glaringly obvious that it is the belief that we can continue with the global capitalist model that is unrealistic. In the crude language of mainstream economists, rational, self-maximizing, utility-seeking individuals are creating the conditions for their own demise and they are doing this in a most efficient manner. Given this reality, why the lack of protest? Why are we not taking to the streets in droves to save ourselves? People certainly are taking to the streets in the South as the ongoing protests against neoliberalism, and the election of anti-neoliberal governments in Venezuela, Bolivia and Ecuador demonstrate. But in the global North, as environmental activist George Monbiot points out:

It appears to be easier to persuade people to protest against the termination of a favourite theme tune, or the loss of imperial measures, or, for that matter, against speed cameras and high fuel prices, than to confront a threat to our existence. There is an obvious reason for this: In those cases, something is being done to us. In this case, we are doing it to ourselves. ... We are simply too comfortable and we have too much to lose.[4]

While Monbiot is referring to the environmentally unsustainable nature of consumer capitalism in the North, he could also have been addressing the challenge of overcoming the socio-economic inequalities inherent in the global capitalist system. After all, our consumer lifestyle in the North is not only made possible by the overt physical violence that results from military interventions around the world, it is itself a source of structural violence—poverty, hunger, crime, disease, limited access to education and many other avoidable social maladies imposed on the South. According to Sue McGregor, a professor of education at Mount St. Vincent University in Halifax, Nova Scotia:

Under the spell of consumerism, few people give thought to whether their consumption habits produce class inequality, alienation, or repressive power, i.e., structural violence. People are concerned more with the "stuff of life" rather than with "quality of life," least of all the quality of life of those producing the goods they consume. Indeed, consumerism is manifested in chronic purchasing of new goods and services with little attention to their true need, durability, country of origin, working conditions, or environmental consequences of manufacture and disposal.[5]

The maintenance of our consumer lifestyle depends on obscuring the links between the comfortable habits of the capitalist consumer in the North and the misery of those in the South who produce the goods. As McGregor points out:

We teach children capitalistic consumerism, yet tell them nothing about the lives of the workers who slave to assemble designer clothing, toys, and electronics; nor the animals that suffered to create fashion or food; nor the environmental impact of the trash we create. And, by no means do we tell them that these situations are inextricably linked.[6]

It is an inevitable fact of global capitalism that our consumption habits in the North are inextricably linked to both environmental devastation and the structural violence imposed on peoples of the South. This realization makes it apparent that the struggle in the North to achieve a more sustainable and egalitarian society is a fight, not for "more," but for "less." According to Monbiot, "It is a campaign not for abundance but for austerity. It is a campaign not for more freedom but for less. Strangest of all, it is a campaign not just against other people, but also against ourselves."[7]

Consequently, the only response to the unsustainable model of global capitalism is for us to wage a revolution within ourselves. First, we must revolutionize the way we think. And then, we must revolutionize the way we live. The principal obstacle to convincing people in the North to become engaged in such a revolution is the strongly held belief that their happiness is directly linked to their materially comfortable lifestyle. In other words, if people in the North were to experience a reduction in their level of material comfort, then they would not be as happy. However, recent studies have suggested that income doesn't correlate with happiness once earnings surpass the amount required to subsist—approximately $15,000 per person, per year, according to Richard Layard, director of the Well-Being Programme at the London School of Economics. As Layard notes:

> Over the last 50 years, living standards in the West have improved enormously but we have become no happier. This shows we should not sacrifice human relationships, which are the main source of happiness, for the sake of economic growth.[8]

Yet, under neoliberalism, sacrificing human relationships—rupturing and dislocating families and communities—is exactly what we have done in our quest for greater levels of material comfort.

So, if people living in wealthy capitalist societies are no happier today than they were half-a-century ago despite dramatic increases in income, why do they continually strive to earn more money to purchase more things? Part of the problem is linked to the concept of "relative deprivation," which argues that it is not only poverty that breeds discontent, but also our perception that our social status is lower than that of our neighbour or others in our society. Layard quotes Karl Marx in order to illustrate this concept: "A house may be large or small; as long as the surrounding houses are equally small, it satisfies all social demands for a dwelling. But if a palace rises beside the little house, the little house shrinks into a hut."[9]

People in the North tend to compare themselves with their wealthier compatriots to determine how well they are doing socially and economically, but no matter how much they improve their own level of material comfort, there are always others who are better off in a capitalist system. The same concept of relative deprivation applies in the South, not only with regard to people comparing themselves to their wealthy neighbours in that part of the world, but also through comparisons with the wealthy nations of the North. Consequently, the false promise of capitalist development remains a powerful motivator. Ultimately then, the perpetual quest to achieve ever-higher levels of material comfort under global capitalism is not only environmentally unsustainable, it is also spiritually unfulfilling because it fails to increase our happiness. In this light, the resident of Las Gaviotas exhibited an impressive degree of enlightenment when he declared: "We believe austerity is a better path to happiness than too much comfort."

The history of capitalism is primarily a history of the struggle between the haves and the have-nots. Under neoliberal globalization, economic elites in both the North and South have once again increased their share of the wealth at the expense of the majority. And while the quality of life for most in the North has deteriorated under globalization, much of the population still enjoys a relatively high level of material comfort when compared with the majority of people in the South. In other words, under globalization, a significant portion of the population of the North constitutes, to varying degrees, the haves, while the majority in the South represent the have-nots—with little hope of improving their lot. And, despite the "free trade" and "free market" rhetoric repeatedly used by neoliberals, capitalism remains an economic system marked by government intervention—to the advantage of the capitalist elites. As a result, William I. Robinson argues:

> The current epoch is a time of rapidly growing global social polarization between a shrinking minority of haves and an expanding majority of have-nots. It is a time of escalating political and military conflict as contending social forces face each other in innumerable yet interwoven struggles around the world. The global capitalist system faced at the turn of the century a structural crisis in overaccumulation and also expanding crisis of legitimacy in the face of the "irresistible" rise of a global justice movement.[10]

Ultimately, the alternative to global capitalism will not be a return to the protectionist measures of the Keynesian era. After all, that industrial model was also rooted in the profit motive and was as environmentally unsustainable as neoliberalism is today. Nor will it lie in the establishment of some form of industrial socialism, which is equally as unsustainable as industrial capitalism. The emergence of a viable alternative model will require radically re-evaluating our values and lifestyles, as well as shedding the widespread apathy that currently permeates our political culture—an apathy that capitalist elites depend on, in conjunction with a process of socialization, to preserve their hegemony. Consequently, while reducing levels of consumption in the North is an essential component of revolutionizing the global socio-economic order, such an individualistic response is hardly sufficient and might result in even greater hardship over the short term for those workers in the South who produce the goods consumed in the North. Self-awareness in the individual must also be linked to, as previously mentioned, collective action at the local, national and international levels if we are to establish the structural conditions favourable to the creation of a more egalitarian and environmentally sustainable society on a global scale. When all of us in Cape Breton, Colombia and beyond finally grasp this reality, the revolution in the way we think will have occurred. All that will then remain will be to revolutionize the way we live. At that point, another world will not only be possible, it will be inevitable.

Epilogue

At the end of 2008, the global capitalist system was in a state of crisis. The international financial system teetered on the brink of collapse, multinational corporations were receiving massive government bailouts, Wall Street indexes were plummeting and millions of workers worldwide had lost their jobs. While much has been written about official responses to this crisis, there is little analysis of the root causes. In short, the implementation of neoliberalism over the past quarter century lies at the root of the current crisis of global capitalism. Once again, people and communities are being economically and socially devastated by the consequences of decisions made in the distant financial centres of the global capitalist system. And, at the same time that millions are becoming unemployed, national governments are scrambling to find a way to address the resulting social crisis after more than two decades of neoliberalism has dismantled much of the social safety net.

The most recent cracks in the global capitalist system appeared in 2007, in what has become known as the sub-prime mortgage crisis.[1] During that year, more than 100 mortgage companies went out of business in the United States and tens of thousands of workers lost their jobs due to the inability of borrowers to meet their debt obligations.[2] Because the U.S. Congress began allowing commercial banks and investment banks to merge with each other in the late 1990s, the liquidity problems experienced by commercial banks as a result of the sub-prime mortgage crisis quickly spread to investment firms. In July 2007, after hitting an all-time high, the Dow Jones Industrial Average began a slow decline over the next year before plummeting on September 15, 2008 when the investment bank Lehman Brothers declared bankruptcy. Uncertainty reigned in the ensuing days as Merrill Lynch was forced to merge with Bank of America in order to ensure its survival and the Bush administration provided an $85 billion bailout to insurance giant American International Group (AIG) in an effort to stabilize the markets.[3] But the markets continued to fall, and by the end of the year the U.S. Congress had approved a $700 billion bailout for the financial sector.

The U.S. economy began to contract rapidly as many consumers discovered that they were over-burdened with debt, while others found it increasingly difficult to access credit from wary banks. Because the capitalist economy is based on high-levels of consumption, which in turn is reliant on American consumers borrowing money in order to continually purchase goods, the so-called credit crunch resulted in an economic crisis. Reduced levels of consumption inevitably led to diminished demand for goods, which then led to a decline in production and eventually to job losses.

After more than two decades of attempting to undermine the security of workers in the global North through the implementation of a global capitalist system that allowed for downsizing and the exporting of jobs to the global South, capitalist elites were suddenly using the fact that thousands of jobs would be lost if they went out of business to justify the need for government bailouts. Indeed, job losses were occurring at a staggering rate. In November 2008, the United States suffered its sharpest one-month drop in employment since 1974 when more than half a million Americans lost their jobs—and for many of them, their health insurance too—bringing the total number of people who had become unemployed that year to almost two million.[4] Meanwhile, many workers and retirees watched helplessly as the value of their pension plans plummeted along with the Dow Jones Industrial Average. Capitalist elites desperately sought to re-establish the consumer confidence that the market relies on, highlighting the insecurity of an economic system that is as much, if not more, reliant on the illusion of stability than actual stability.

Because of the prominent role played by the United States in the global capitalist system, the financial crisis—coupled with declining levels of consumption—soon saw the economic downturn spread to other countries and the world quickly found itself heading towards its worst depression in more than 70 years. Even emerging economic superpower China was not immune to the crisis as the global downturn significantly slowed its rate of economic growth in 2008. More than 87,000 Chinese factories closed in the first six months of the year and that number was expected to surpass 100,000 by early 2009.[5]

In response to the global crisis, leaders of many European nations and other economic powers also began devising bailouts and stimulus plans to jump-start their economies and to partially replenish social programs that had been seriously undermined by neoliberalism. By the end of 2008, Britain had committed to investing $418 billion, Germany $213 billion, Japan $275 billion and China $600 billion into their economies.[6] Throughout the industrialized world, pro-neoliberal governments were rapidly resorting to Keynesian interventionism by engaging in deficit spending in order to stimulate their economies. There was only one industrialized nation in late 2008 that remained true to its neoliberal beliefs and resistant to a Keynesian-style response. That country was Canada.

In mid-September, despite the collapse of Lehman Brothers and the corresponding plunge in the financial markets, Prime Minister Harper appeared to be in denial of the magnitude of the economic crisis when he declared, "My own belief is if we were going to have some kind of crash or recession, we probably would have had it by now."[7] The following month, Canada experienced its worst one-month job loss in 26 years as 71,000 workers were made redundant. According to Scotia Capital economist Derek Holt, "Deteriorating global job markets have arrived on Canada's doorstep such that the country is no longer bucking the general trend of lost jobs in most major economies."[8]

In November, Harper joined President Bush and other world leaders at the Asian Pacific Economic Co-operation (APEC) summit in Lima, Peru. Talks at the summit were dominated by the global economic recession and Harper finally acknowledged that the world was facing its worst crisis since the Wall Street crash of 1929. However, the Canadian prime minister urged the other 20 leaders in attendance to stay the neoliberal course and to avoid resorting to Keynesian policies in order to address the crisis, declaring, "Removing protectionist barriers and easing trade restrictions was a big factor in ushering in this extraordinary [neoliberal] era. We cannot allow ourselves to turn back."[9] And, contrary to conventional wisdom, Harper went on to claim that the introduction of regulatory and protectionist policies actually prolonged the Great Depression.

In the summit's final declaration, the twenty-one leaders vowed to avoid protectionism and to maintain a global free market system. They also declared that the crisis would be over by 2010.[10] In reality, some of the world's most powerful economic nations had somewhat contradictorily decided to implement Keynesian-style economic stimulus packages in an attempt to jump-start the global economy while simultaneously espousing neoliberal ideals such as the maintaining of a global free trade system. Harper illustrated his ongoing commitment to neoliberalism at the summit by signing a free trade agreement with Colombia's President Uribe.[11]

But what lies at the root of the global economic crisis? Former chief economist for the World Bank and Nobel laureate Joseph Stiglitz is one of the most prominent mainstream economists to have addressed this question. Stiglitz, who advocates a more Keynesian approach, claims that the problem is "a belief that markets are self-adjusting and that the role of government should be minimal."[12] It was the shift from the Keynesian model to neoliberalism that occurred in the United States under the Reagan administration that led to the dismantling of the regulatory framework established as a response to the Great Depression. Stiglitz argues that the first in a series of fatal decisions in the financial sector was President Reagan's appointment of Alan Greenspan as president of the Federal Reserve Board in 1987. The Federal Reserve is responsible for ensuring the stability of the financial system, which inevitably means regulating the investment and banking sectors. However, according to Stiglitz, Greenspan was appointed because "Reagan wanted someone who did not believe any such thing, and he found in him a devotee of the objectivist philosopher and free-market zealot Ayn Rand."[13] Greenspan quickly became the darling of capitalist elites as he helped ensure the entrenchment of the free market philosophy in government fiscal policy.

The process of financial deregulation initiated under Greenspan's watch led to the U.S. Congress repealing the Glass-Steagall Act in November 1999 following a $300 million lobbying effort by banking and investment firms. According to Stiglitz, "Glass-Steagall had long separated commercial banks (which lend money) and investment banks (which organize the sale of bonds and equities); it had been enacted in the aftermath of the Great Depression and was meant to curb the excesses of that era, including grave conflicts of interest."[14] The repeal of Glass-Steagall led to an increase in the number of relatively conservative commercial banks that began seeking higher returns through high-risk investments. Another contributing factor to the crisis was the decision by the Securities and Exchange Commission in 2004 to allow large investment banks to increase their debt-to-capital ratio from 12:1 to 30:1 so they could buy more mortgage-backed securities. This decision further inflated the housing bubble, which eventually burst when the sub-prime mortgage crisis hit and home foreclosures skyrocketed.[15] The result was a credit crunch for millions of Americans who were dependent on their credit cards and home equity loans to meet their monthly financial obligations.

Greenspan himself acknowledged that the neoliberal model was flawed when he was called to testify before Congressional hearings into the crisis in October 2008. When asked if his ideological beliefs led him to make regulatory decisions as president of the Federal Reserve that he would later regret, Greenspan replied, "Yes, I've found a flaw. I don't know how significant or permanent it is. But I've been very distressed by that fact."[16]

One significant flaw in the system is the fact that the massive rates of consumption—particularly in the global North—required to sustain the global capitalist economy are predicated on consumer access to high levels of credit. In other words, in order to maintain high consumption levels, consumers have to borrow against their future income, primarily through credit cards but also through home equity and other types of loans. As long as people can continue to access credit, and as long as they remain employed and earning a decent wage in order to pay their debts, then the system stays afloat on the premise that tomorrow's earnings will pay for today's consumption. However, as soon as people's access to credit is hindered—whether through more conservative lending practices by financial institutions or the wariness of consumers already overly-burdened with debt—then the resulting reduction in consumption causes the system to crash. The same premise is even more applicable to global capitalism's over-dependence on the unsustainable consumption of the planet's finite resources, particularly fossil fuels.

Serious questions are now being raised in mainstream circles about the sustainability of the model. Financial analyst Manas Chakravarty asks and answers one such question:

> What are policymakers doing to solve this problem created by this explosion of debt? Why, try their best to reopen the casino, urge U.S. consumers to continue spending, flood the markets with

money so that its cost comes down and people start borrowing again. Private debt is being replaced with public debt. They are desperately trying to pump air back into the bubble.[17]

Chakravarty is referring to one of the principal objectives of the Bush administration's bailout of the banking sector, which was to inject liquidity into financial institutions in an effort to increase the amount of credit available to people. In essence, the disease is being offered as the cure. The government sought to stimulate the economy from the grassroots level on up by helping people borrow more money so they can once again increase their levels of consumption in order to get the economy back on track and return corporations to profitability.

Upon assuming office in January 2009, U.S. President Barack Obama quickly formulated a stimulus package to follow-up on the Bush administration's bailout package. Reflecting neoliberal doctrine—and a desire to appease Republicans—tax cuts accounted for almost 40 percent of the $819 billion plan, despite the fact that the government was already running a deficit and there was an increased need to fund an expansion of the social safety net.[18] The newly-elected president also sought to address the economic crisis by advocating traditional Keynesian policies including increased funding for education and health care as well as a "Buy American" provision that many capitalist elites immediately labelled as a protectionist measure. Obama's plan also sought to further intervene in the economy by funding the largest public works program in more than half a century. In order to create jobs, Obama planned to implement a 21st century version of President Franklin Delano Roosevelt's Keynesian-influenced New Deal, which was a response to the Great Depression. Obama's stimulus plan intended to use federal taxpayer dollars to make public buildings more energy efficient, rebuild the nation's highways and bridges, renovate aging school buildings, improve technology in schools and to modernize hospitals, among other things.

The same month, the Harper government announced its budget, which begrudgingly included an economic stimulus plan offering just enough incentives to ensure that the Liberals supported it. The $35 billion stimulus package was one of the smallest—in ratio to GDP— among the world's industrialized nations and was even lower than the amount recommended by the IMF. It mostly adhered to neoliberal doctrine by calling for broad-based tax cuts as an incentive to rejuvenate consumer spending. The Conservatives flirted with Keynesianism to the degree that the budget would ensure the government would not be brought down in a vote of no confidence. The budget only provided token additional funding for the country's unemployment program and failed to loosen eligibility requirements, thereby condemning increasing numbers of unemployed Canadians to further economic hardship. It promised a significant amount for much-needed infrastructure projects, but cash-strapped provinces were required to produce the up-front money before they could receive federal funds, ensuring that many essential projects would not be undertaken and the stimulus affect would be nullified. In short, the Harper government only wavered from its neoliberal mantra to the degree that was necessary to ensure its political survival. As Hugh MacKenzie, an economist at the Canadian Center for Policy Alternatives, pointed out, "It is brutally obvious that the Harper government has been dragged by political imperative into a set of budgetary policies that it considers to be ideologically unpalatable—a necessary evil to be pursued for its political value alone, implemented in half measures and abandoned as quickly as possible."[19]

The Harper government's budget offered little for the poorest sectors of Canadian society and, as usually occurs in recessions, it is the poor who are most negatively affected by the economic crisis. Similarly, the poor in nations of the global South are also being forced to endure even more economic hardship, including higher levels of hunger, malnutrition and other social maladies related to their socio-economic status—because poverty is one thing that does "trickle down" under global capitalism. In places such as Cape Breton and Colombia, which exist on the periphery of the global economic system and are heavily dependent on remittances sent back by their exported population, the money flow has decreased significantly as workers have become unemployed.[20] Furthermore, some of those unemployed workers will return home and exert an even greater strain on fragile social safety nets.

Perhaps the only short-term benefit of the global recession is that oil prices have plummeted. The sharp decline in manufacturing output—and the consequent reduction in the amount of goods being shipping around the globe—along with the collapse of speculative futures trading on Wall Street diminished demand for oil and drove prices down. As a result, global oil prices had dropped below $50 a barrel by the end of 2008, thereby making transportation, heating and cooking fuel more affordable for the world's impoverished population. However, the potential negative of this decline is a reduction in incentives to move towards more sustainable and environmentally-friendly energy sources. Inevitably, once economic growth recommences, the price of oil will again resume its upward trajectory.

The current global economic crisis makes evident the fragility of the global capitalist system. It clearly illustrates how capitalism prioritizes profit for a few over sustainable lifestyles for all, including future generations. As the massive bailouts of corporations have once again made evident, neoliberals are not adverse to government intervention when it socializes the losses of capitalist elites through corporate welfare programs. These massive government interventions represent a desperate attempt by capitalist elites—all too willing to contradict their ideological beliefs—to preserve the global capitalist system by avoiding the collapse that would inevitably occur if they played by their own rules. In short, capitalist elites are intent on preserving a global economic system that, at the best of times, has failed to serve the basic needs of more than half the world's population and is predicated on maintaining gross inequalities at the global level.

So what lies ahead? There are essentially two potential outcomes to the crisis. In many ways, we have returned to the juncture we found ourselves in during the 1920s and early 1930s when the future of the global capitalist system lay momentarily in the balance. At that time, capitalist elites in North America and Europe entered into the Fordist compact with the working class while simultaneously introducing a Keynesian policy framework that ensured the preservation of the capitalist model, albeit in a more regulated form. Sadly, it appears that the economic stimulus plans of President Obama, Prime Minister Harper and other world leaders are in the Keynesian vein and are not intended to challenge the fundamental structures of capitalism or to significantly diminish the gross inequalities that exist globally. And, as occurred in the 20th century, the capitalist elites will likely succeed in dismantling the new Keynesian model and implementing some form of neoliberalism. Consequently, history will repeat itself and down the line we will once again find ourselves back in the same dilemma that we are now experiencing. As Stiglitz notes regarding the 20th century shift to neoliberalism, "The embrace by America—and much of the rest of the world—of this flawed economic philosophy made it inevitable that we would eventually arrive at the place we are today."[21]

The second potential outcome involves the establishment of an alternative to the global capitalist model. While Obama's policies do not represent radical change, they do constitute reforms to the global capitalist system and, as U.S. economist Doug Henwood notes, "Back in the Gorbachev days, the anticommunist right loved to quote Tocqueville saying that the riskiest time for a bad regime is when it starts to reform itself. That's where our regime is right now, and it's a good time for us, whoever we are exactly, to go out and make it riskier. It's going to get easier to win recruits as the ranks of the disappointed swell."[22] Consequently, the time is ripe for the "disappointed" to rise up and pressure governments into restructuring their economies to ensure that more sustainable, locally-based production methods and markets replace the existing global free trade system. By redistributing power and wealth from transnational institutions and corporations to the local level, communities could begin to establish more democratic, sustainable and environmentally-friendly alternatives to an unpredictable global capitalist economy that has often failed to address most people's basic needs and has never been accountable to the global citizenry.

The massive amounts of taxpayer money being spent on economic stimulus programs would go a long way towards initiating a far-reaching social, economic and environmental transformation. However, any such revolutionary restructuring of the global capitalist system would have to be demanded by people around the globe. After all, despite acknowledgements by such pro-capitalist luminaries as Stiglitz and Greenspan that the model is flawed, capitalist elites are not about to relinquish their stranglehold on power and wealth without a fight. As the leaders at the APEC summit made clear in their closing statement, they intend to emerge from this economic crisis with the fundamental structures of global capitalism intact. In other words, they intend to ensure that another world is not possible. It is up to us to show that it is.

Notes

Notes to introduction

1. Neoliberalism is an economic philosophy rooted in the concepts of free markets and free trade. Its proponents seek to transfer control over the economy from the state to the private sector. Some of the fundamental tenets of neoliberalism are the privatization of state-owned entities, reduced taxes, fiscal discipline, deregulation, removal of trade barriers and anti-unionism.

2. Robinson, "What is Critical Globalization Studies?" in *Public Sociologies Reader*, 21-36.

Notes to chapter one

1. Murphy, "Hanging Out the Welcome Sign," *Time*, http://www.time.com/time/magazine/article/0,9171,951396-3,00.html.

2. For a more detailed analysis of the Staples Theory. see Harold Innis, *The Cod Fisheries: The History of an International Economy*.

3. Barlow and May, *Frederick Street*, 8.

4. Heron, *Working in Steel*, 31.

5. Ibid., 79-81.

6. Ibid., 82.

7. Ibid., 88.

8. MacEachern, *George MacEachern: An Autobiography*, 18.

9. Heron, 88-89.

10. Ibid., 97.

11. Ibid., 137.

12. Ibid., 144.

13. Interview with author, Sydney, Nova Scotia, 4 September 2007.

14. MacEwan, *Miners and Steelworkers*, 55.

15. Ibid., 53-54.

16. Frank, *J. B. McLachlan: A Biography*, 185.

17. MacEwan, 48.

18. Frank, 187.

19. MacEwan, 73-74.

20. Ibid., 76-77.

21. MacEachern, 22-23.

22. Frank, 296-97.

23. Heron, 153-55.

24. Ibid., 156.

25. Frank, 303.

26. Heron, 158-59.

27. Ibid., 30.

28. Lipton, *The Trade Union Movement of Canada 1827-1959*, 248.

29. Frank, 431.

30. Lipton, 248.

31. Workman, *Social Torment*, 15.

32. Don MacGillivray, "Workers in Cape Breton: Not Really Hot-Heads," *Catholic New Times*, 30 March 1997, 7.

33. Lipton, 238.

34. Kealey, *Workers and Canadian History*, 339.

35. Frank, 178.

36. Lipton, 301.

37. DeRoche, "Culture of Poverty Lives On," *City & Society*, 225-54.

38. MacAuley, "Contradictions in Community Economic Development," in *From the net to the Net*, 115-36.

39. Ibid.

40. Saez and Veall, "The Evolution of High Incomes in Northern America," *The American Economic Review*, 831-49.

41. Lipton, 269.

42. Ibid., 284.

43. By the end of the 20th century Canadian labour, particularly public sector unions, had become highly critical of the neoliberal model and were establishing solidarity with workers in the global South. However, the ideology of most was firmly-rooted in social democratic ideals and few were actively seeking the overthrow of capitalism itself and openly advocating the establishment of some form of socialism.

44. Workman, 39.

45. "Federal Commercialization in Canada," Parliamentary Information and Research Group.

46. Ibid.

47. "Income Inequality and Redistribution in Canada: 1976 to 2004," Statistics Canada, 13.

48. Banting, "Do We Know Where We Are Going?" *Canadian Public Policy*, 421-29.

49. Jeffrey Owens, *Fundamental Tax Reform: The Experience of OECD Countries*, 16.

50. "Canada's New Government is Providing Real Tax Relief for Canadians," Finance Canada.

51. "About CCCE," Canadian Council of Chief Executives.

52. Barlow, *Too Close for Comfort*, 286.

53. DeRoche, 225-54.

54. Bailey and Boyce, "The Manufacturing and Marketing of Steel in Canada," in *Business and Economic History*, 229-36.

55. "Industry Snapshot: Primary Steel in Canada," Industry Canada, 12.

56. Ibid., 17-18.

57. Ibid., 15.

58. Ibid., 20.

59. Macklem, "A Steel City's Blues," *Maclean's*, 31.

60. Lateline, "FTA is Not Free or Fair, Says Hargrove."

61. Macklem, "Shifting Into Reverse," *Maclean's*, 32.

62. "Moving to Address High Cancer Rates in Cape Breton," Nova Scotia, Department of Health.

63. Barlow and May, 1-2.

64. *2004 Annual Financial Report*, Emera, 14.

Notes to chapter two

1. One example is the FENSUAGRO peasant union federation, which has eighty thousand members and continues to provide support, guidance and human rights protection to rural workers throughout Colombia.

2. Juarez, "Trade and Development Policies in Colombia," *Studies in Comparative and International Development*, 67-97.

3. Bush, George H.W. "Statement on Trade Initiatives for the Andean Region."

4. Clements, "Starbucks Announces Its Earnings Set Record," cited in Garry Leech, *Killing Peace*, 51.

5. *Colombia Poverty Report*, The World Bank Group.

6. *Colombia: En contravía de las recomendaciones internacionales sobre derechos humanos, Balance de la política de seguridad democrática y la situación de derechos humanos y derecho humanitario, agosto 2002 a agosto 2004*, Colombian Commission for Jurists.

7. Interview with author, Riohacha, La Guajira, Colombia, 9 August 2006.

8. Ramírez Cuellar, *The Profits of Extermination*, 32.

9. *El Embrujo Autoritario: Primer Año de Gobierno de Álvaro Uribe Vélez*, Plataforma Colombiana de Derechos Humanos, Democracia y Desarollo.

10. Uribe, "Palabras del Presidente Uribe en posesión de nuevo comandante de la FAC."

11. Annual Survey of Violations of Trade Union Rights – 2006, International Confederation of Trade Unions (ICFTU).

12. Moberg, "Stuck in the Middle," *In These Times*, http://www.inthesetimes.com/article/582/.

13. Flóres, "Migration and the Urban Informal Sector in Colombia" (conference paper).

14. Mesa Toro and Reina Salgado, "Notes on Economic and Labor Factors in Colombia 2005," National Union School.

15. "Minister: IMF, Multilateral Banks Have Impoverished Latin America," Hoover's Online, cited in Garry Leech, *Killing Peace*, 52.

16. For more information about Colombia's oil reforms, see Garry Leech, *Crude Interventions*.

17. "Entrevista con José Armando Zamora, director de la ANH," *Carta Petrolera*, http://www.ecopetrol.com.co/especiales/carta/entrevista.htm.

18. Higgs, "The Trillion-Dollar Defense Budget Is Already Here."

19. Isacson, "The 2000-2001 Colombia Aid Package By the Numbers."

20. Spokesperson for Occidental Petroleum, interview with author, Bogotá, Colombia, 10 February 2003.

21. Interview with author, Orito, Putumayo, Colombia, 2 March 2004.

22. Ibid.

23. Indira A. R. Lakshmanan, "$4 Billion Later, Drugs Still Flow in Colombia," *Boston Globe*, 21 May 2006. http://www.boston.com/news/world/latinamerica/articles/2006/05/21/4b_later_drugs_still_flow_in_colombia/.

24. Ramírez Cuellar, 87.

25. Ibid., 85-86.

26. Russell Hubbard, "Drummond Unearths its Future in Colombia," *Birmingham News*, 9 April 2006, 1A.

27. David Bacon, "U.S. Fuels Dirty War Against Unions," *Green Left Weekly*, 8 August 2001. http://www.greenleft.org.au/2001/459/25524.

28. Frank Bajak, "U.S. Coal Firm Linked to Colombia Militias," *Washington Post*, 6 July 2007. http://www.washingtonpost.com/wp-dyn/content/article/2007/07/06/AR2007070601630.html.

29. Ibid.

30. Interview with author, La Loma, Cesar, Colombia, 6 August 2006.

31. Matt Apuzzo, "Chiquita Pleads Guilty in Terror Probe," *Washington Post*, 19 March 2007. http://www.washingtonpost.com/wp-dyn/content/article/2007/03/19/AR2007031900641_pf.html.

32. Amnesty International, *Colombia: The Paramilitaries in Medellín: Demobilization or Legalization?*, 2005

33. U.S. Office on Colombia, *Paramilitary Demobilization*, n.d.

34. Interview with author, Riohacha, La Guajira, Colombia, 9 August 2006.

35. *Colombia 2002-2006: Situación de derechos humanos y derecho humanitario*, Comisión Colombiano de Juristas.

36. Interview with author, La Jagua de Ibirico, Cesar, Colombia, 5 August 2006.

37. Interview with author, Valledupar, Cesar, Colombia, 8 August 2006.

38. Interview with author, La Loma, Cesar, Colombia, 6 August 2006.

39. "Community," Drummond Company, Inc.

40. Ramírez Cuellar, 55-62

41. Ibid., 63.

42. Chris Arsenault, "Colombia: Foreign Firms Cashing in on Generous Mining Code," Inter Press Service, 22 October 2007. http://ipsnews.net/news.asp?idnews=39755.

43. Ibid.

44. Newell, "Citizenship, Accountability and Community," *International Affairs*, 541-57.

45. Chomsky, *Linked Labor Histories*, 266.

46. Ibid., 276.

47. Ibid., 277.

48. Interview with author, Albania, La Guajira, Colombia, 13 August 2002.

49. Interview with author, Hatonuevo, La Guajira, Colombia, 13 May 2005.

50. Interview with author, Riohacha, La Guajira, 14 August 2002.

51. Email interview with author, September 2002.

52. Disclaimer: The authors were engaged in the campaign waged by the Atlantic Regional Solidarity Network (ARSN) to raise awareness of the human rights issues related to Nova Scotia Power's importation of Colombian coal.

53. Telephone interview with author, Sydney, Nova Scotia, December 2004.

54. Chomsky, 283.

55. Exchange witnessed by authors, Halifax, Nova Scotia, 24 March 2006.

56. Bennett, "Resisting Corporate Power in Colombia."

57. C169 Indigenous and Tribal Peoples Convention, 1989, International Labour Organisation.

58. Shiva, "New Emperors, Old Clothes."

59. MacNeil, "Reflections on Mining in Colombia."

60. Ibid.

61. Interview with author, Riohacha, La Guajira, Colombia, 9 August 2006.

62. Canadian Press, "Ship Belonging to PM's Son Raided for Drugs," *Globe and Mail*, 1 July 2004. http://www.theglobeandmail.com/servlet/story/RT-GAM.20040701.wcsl0701/BNStory/Na.

Notes to chapter three

1. "2006 Census of Canada: Nova Scotia Perspective," Nova Scotia Department of Finance.

2. "Labour Market Review 2004 – Cape Breton," Service Canada.

3. "Annual Labour Market Perspectives – Cape Breton 2006," Service Canada.

4. Ibid.

5. *Moving in the Right Direction? Labour Mobility, Labour Shortage and Canada's Human Potential*, Action Canada.

6. "Nova Scotia Labour Market – December 2005," Nova Scotia Department of Finance.

7. Steedman, "The Changing Face of the Call Centre Industry in Canada."

8. Competitive Alternatives: KPMG's Guide to International Business Costs, KPMG.

9. Rodney MacDonald, "A Great Place to Do Business, Indeed," *Chronicle Herald*, 27 March 2006. http://www.gov.ns.ca/premier/speeches/2006-03-27GreatPlacet-odoBusiness.asp.

10. Bickerton and MacNeil, "Models of Development for Atlantic Canada," in *Doing Development Differently*, 42-71.

11. Good and McFarland, "Call Centres," in *From the net to the Net*, 99-113.

12. Ibid., 111.

13. "Xerox to Build New TeleWeb Centre in Halifax." Presswire. 25 September 2001. Online at Access My Library. http://www.accessmylibrary.com/coms2/summary_0286-10400666_ITM.

14. Ibid.

15. Bruce Erskine, "American Call Centres Feeling Pinch of High Canadian Dollar," *The Chronicle Herald*, 27 February 2008, C3.

16. Roger Taylor, "Finding a Way to Compete with Our Dollar at Par," *The Chronicle Herald*, 27 February 2008, C1-3.

17. Tanya Collier MacDonald, "Province Answers ServiCom's Call," *Cape Breton Post*, 16. April 2007. http://www.capebretonpost.com/index.cfm?sid=23327&sc=145.

18. Canadian Press, "Paragon Advanced of Bermuda to Expand Halifax IT Centre," *Cape Breton Post*, 29 October 2007. http://www.capebretonpost.com/index.cfm?sid=75425&sc=145.

19. Workman, 72.

20. Ibid., 72.

21. *Socio-Economic Impact Analysis of the Tele-Service Industry on Cape Breton Island, Canmac Economics*, 6-7.

22. "2001 Poverty Lines," Canadian Council on Social Development.

23. Interview with author, Sydney, Nova Scotia, 17 February 2008. Richard MacNeil is not the interviewee's real name. He requested that his real name not be used because EDS has warned employees not to talk about their job.

24. Ibid.

25. "Project Information Site," Enterprise Cape Breton Corporation. See also, "Stream to Establish 900-Job Centre at Glace Bay," Enterprise Cape Breton Corporation.

26. Macklem, "A Steel City's Blues," *Maclean's*, 31.

27. Ibid., 31-32.

28. Daniel MacIsaac, "Dell Puts the Call Out," *Edmonton Sun*, 1 February 2008. http://www.edmontonsun.com/News/Edmonton/2008/02/01/4805563-sun.html.

29. David Finlayson, "900 Jobs Lost As Dell Bolts," *Edmonton Journal*, 1 February 2008. http://www.canada.com/edmontonjournal/story.html?id=6b890d8b-f0fd-4bf6-903a-e834860ab375&k=47529.

30. Erskine, 32.

31. *2006 Annual Report*, Wal-Mart Stores, Inc., 18.

32. Adams, "Organizing Wal-Mart," Just Labour, 1-11.

33. Ibid.

34. "Canada Fact Sheet," Wal-Mart Stores, Inc.

35. Adams.

36. Bianco, "No Union Please, We're Wal-Mart," *Business Week*, http://www. businessweek.com/magazine/content/06_07/b3971115.htm.

37. Kennedy, Fish Plant Workers Responding to Globalization in North Sydney, *Cape Breton Post*, 1.

38. Julie Collins, "Forty Workers Laid Off at Clearwater," *Cape Breton Post*, 15 October 2005, B4.

39. Ibid., A1.

40. The Canadian Press, "Workers at Clearwater Fish Plant in N.S. Vote to Accept Offer, End Lockout," *The Daily News*, 7 April 2007.

41. *Strategies for the Long Term*, Clearwater Seafoods.

42. Leatherdale, "The Bell Tolls."

43. *BP Statistical Review of World Energy 2007*, BP.

44. "Monthly U.S. Crude Oil and Petroleum Products Imports from Canada," Energy Information Administration.

45. "Canada and the North American Free Trade Agreement," Foreign Affairs and International Trade Canada.

46. Ibid.

47. LeFort, "Energy Revenues."

48. Juan Forero, "In Venezuela, a Face-Off Over the Prospect of Oil Riches," *International Herald Tribune*, 1 June 2006. http://www.iht.com/articles/2006/06/01/business/oil.php.

49. The Pembina Institute. "Misdirected Spending."

50. LeFort. Also, royalties and most corporate income taxes are collected at the provincial level in Canada, as opposed to at the national level in Norway and most other oil-rich nations.

51. Ibid.

52. Associated Press, "ExxonMobil Posts $40.6 Billion Annual Profit," MSNBC, 1 February 2008. http://www.msnbc.msn.com/id/22949325/.

53. Dyer et al. "Under-Mining the Environment."

54. Russell Gold, "As Prices Soar, Oil Giants Turn Sludge Into Gold," *Wall Street Journal*, in the Pittsburgh Post-Gazette, 28 March 2006. http://www.post-gazette.com/pg/06087/677525-28.stm.

55. Lustgarten, "The Dark Magic of Oil Sands," Fortune, http://money.cnn.com/magazines/fortune/fortune_archive/2005/10/03/8356746/index.htm.

56. Dyer et al. "Under-Mining the Environment."

57. Sinclair, *Atlantica: Myths and Reality*.

58. Ibid.

59. Ibid.

60. David Ebner, "Newfoundland's New Plan Focuses On Ownership Stake," *Globe and Mail*, 12 September 2007, B6.

61. Kohler, "Danny Williams Picks His Battles," *Maclean's*, http://www.macleans. ca/canada/national/article.jsp?content=20060731_130820_130820.

62. Dodds and Colman, "Income Distribution in Nova Scotia, 2000," in *From the net to the Net*, 79-80.

63. Heisz, "Income Inequality and Redistribution in Canada: 1976 to 2004," Statistics Canada, May 2007, 6.

64. Ibid., 19.

65. Ibid., 10.

66. Ibid., 9.

67. Ibid., 14.

68. Saez and Veall, "The Evolution of High Incomes in Northern America," *The American Economic Review*, 831-49.

69. Ibid.

70. Sacouman, "Capitalist Restructuring on Canada's East Coast," in *From the net to the Net*, 60.

71. Barlow, *Too Close for Comfort*, 16.

72. Ferguson, *The Potential of Private Sector Health Care in Canada*.

73. Ibid.

74. Ibid.

75. Gulli and Lunau, "Adding Fuel to the Doctor Crisis," *Maclean's*, http://www. macleans.ca/science/health/article.jsp?content=20080102_122329_6200.

76. Jonathan Spicer, "GST Cut Likely the Last, Harper Says," Reuters, in the *National Post*, 31 December 2007. http://www.financialpost.com/story. html?id=208484.

77. John Donnelly, "47 Million Americans Are Uninsured," *Boston Globe*, 29 August 2007. http://www.boston.com/news/nation/articles/2007/08/29/47_million_americans_are_uninsured/.

78. "University Tuition Fees," Statistics Canada, 18 October 2007.

79. Robinson.

80. "UCCB and NSCC Partnership Continues to Export Petroleum Training Expertise to Other Parts of the World," Cape Breton University, 6 August 2004. http://www.cbu.ca/cbu/newsrel/NewsDetail.asp?NewsID=33.

81. "IMPACT Fund: Investment Management of Portfolios in Atlantic Canada Training," IMPACT Fund.

82. Ibid.

83. "Letter from the Dean," IMPACT Fund.

84. Olgilve, *From Public U to Private U*.

85. Ibid.

86. Fredrik Jansson, interview with author, Stockholm, Sweden, 17 November 2006.

87. *Human Development Report 2006*, United Nations Development Programme.

88. David Johnson, "If We Have Free Health Care, Why Not Free University Tuition," *Cape Breton Post*, April 26, 2006, A4.

89. The Vanier Institute of the Family, *The Current State of Canadian Family Finances – 2007 Report*.

90. Ibid.

91. Ibid.

92. Ibid.

93. "Survey of Financial Security – 2005" Statistics Canada.

94. Interview with author, Sydney, Nova Scotia, 30 October 2008.

95. "ECBC Program Guidelines," Enterprise Cape Breton Corporation.

96. "Cape Breton Luxury Resort Gets $1M Boost from ECBC," CBC News, 28 March 2008. http://www.cbc.ca/canada/novascotia/story/2008/03/28/louisbourg-ecbc.html.

97. MacAuley, "Contradictions in Community Economic Development," in *From the net to the Net*, 116.

98. DeRoche, 225-254.

99. Interview with author, Sydney, Nova Scotia, 3 November 2008.

100. MacAuley, 116.

101. DeRoche, 225-254.

102. DeRoche, 225-254.

Notes to chapter four

1. "Human Rights Trump Free Trade for Canadians," *Angus Reid Global Monitor*.

2. Canadian Post "Harper Announces Start of Free Trade Talks with Colombia and Peru," *Edmonton Sun*, 16 July 2007. http://www.edmontonsun.com/News/Canada/2007/07/16/4344203.html.

3. For more information about the consequences of neoliberalism in Venezuela, see Garry Leech, *Crude Interventions*.

4. "Venezuela: Country Report on Human Rights Practices for 1998." U.S. Department of State, 26 February 1999.

5. "Decreta con Fuerza de Ley Organica de Hidrocarburos," *Gaceta Oficial de la República Bolivariana de Venezuela*.

6. Ibid. See also, Bernard Mommer, "Subversive Oil," in *Venezuelan Politics in the Chávez Era*, 141.

7. David J. Lynch, "Oil—Venezuela's Lifeblood—Is Also a Political Flashpoint," *USA Today*, 4 April 2007. http://www.usatoday.com/money/world/2007-04-04-venezuela-1b-usat_N.htm.

8. Brian Ellsworth, "Harvest Accepts Oil Deal," *Houston Chronicle*, 6 August 2005. http://www.chron.com/disp/story.mpl/business/3298656.html.

9. Lynch.

10. For more on the implications of the Chávez's government's Bolivarian revolution for democracy in Latin America in the neoliberal era, see Terry Gibbs, "Business as Unusual."

11. Hugo Chávez, "Do We Want to End Poverty? Let Us Empower the Poor (The Venezuelan Experience)," speech given at the UN Meeting of Heads of State, September 2004.

12. Lisandro Perez, interview with author, Barrio 23 de Enero, Caracas, 29 April 2005.

13. Ibid.

14. Francisco Armada, interview with author, Caracas, Venezuela, 18 May 2005.

15. Ibid.

16. "Cuba, Venezuela Sign Oil Deal," Associated Press, 30 October 2000. http://www.latinamericanstudies.org/venezuela/oil-deal.htm.

17. Francisco Armada, interview with author.

18. Ibid.

19. Maybarduk, "A Peoples Health System."

20. Anonymous, interview with author, 29 April 2005, Caracas, Venezuela.

21. Tibisay Miranda, interview with author, 17 May 2005, Caracas, Venezuela.

22. Lisandro Perez, interview with author.

23. Francisco Armada, interview with author.

24. Instituto Nacional de Estadística, Gobierno Bolivariano de Venezuela, http://www.ocei.gov.ve/condiciones/educacion.asp. Accessed 19 September 2005.

25. Arnaldo Sotillo, director, Escuela Basica Integral Bolivariana Estado Vargas, interview with author, 17 May 2005, Caracas, Venezuela.

26. Ibid.

27. Luisa Ruiz, interview with author, 19 May 2005, Caracas, Venezuela.

28. Arreaza, "ALBA: Bolivarian Alternative for Latin America and the Caribbean."

29. "The Resignation of Rafael Correa, Ecuador's Economy Minister: An Example of IFIs Influence?" IFIs Latin American Monitor, 22 August 2005, http://ifis.choike.org/informes/123.html.

30. Mark Tran, "Venezuela Quits IMF and World Bank," *The Guardian*, 1 May 2007, http://www.guardian.co.uk/business/2007/may/01/venezuela.imf.

31. Alexei Barrionuevo, "Chávez's Plan for Development Bank Moves Ahead," *The New York Times*, 21 October 2007, http://www.nytimes.com/2007/10/22/world/americas/22bank.html?_r=1&oref=slogin.

32. "El Banco del Sur arrancará con US$10.000 millones," *La Nación*, 27 June 2008, http://www.lanacion.com.ar/nota.asp?nota_id=1025281.

33. "Caribbean Oil Initiative Launched," BBC News, 30 June 2005, http://news.bbc.co.uk/2/hi/americas/4636067.stm.

34. Weisbrot, "Poverty Reduction in Venezuela: A Reality-Based View," ReVista: *Harvard Review of Latin America*, 1-8.

35. Shiva, *Earth Democracy*, 32-33.

36. Broadhead, *International Environmental Politics*, 95.

37. Bush, George W. "Press Conference of the President," 20 December 2006.

38. Bush, George W. "Press Conference of the President," 28 February 2008.

39. Broadhead, 149.

40. Hull, "The Role of Geology in the Management of Ohio's Solid Waste." http://www.dnr.state.oh.us/geosurvey/gen/environment/Manage/tabid/7913/Default.aspx.

41. Straszheim, "The Economic Impact of Growth in China," *CFA Institute Conference Proceedings Quarterly*, 88-93.

42. Seth Kaplan, "Haves and Have-nots: China's Boom Leaves Many Behind," *International Herald Tribune*, 26 March 2004. http://www.iht.com/articles/2004/03/26/edkaplan_ed3_.php.

43. Flannery, *The Weather Makers*, 74.

44. Ibid., 275.

45. Yao, "China's Oil Strategy and Its Implications for U.S.-China Relations," *Issues and Studies*, 165-201.

46. Adam Porter, "'Peak Oil' Enters Mainstream Debate," BBC News, 10 June 2005, http://news.bbc.co.uk/2/hi/business/4077802.stm.

47. Martinez, "Panama: Does Geography Matter?"

48. "Utopia Rises Out of the Colombian Plains," *All Things Considered*, National Public Radio, 29 August 1994. http://www.dharma-haven.org/five-havens/weisman.htm.

49. White and Gonzalez Marino, "Las Gaviotas: Sustainability in the Tropics," *World Watch Magazine*.

50. "Utopia Rises Out of the Colombian Plains," *All Things Considered*.

51. Weisman, "Colombia's Model City." *Context: A Quarterly of Humane Sustainable Culture*. http://www.context.org/ICLIB/IC42/Colombia.htm.

52. White and Gonzalez Marino.

53. Weisman.

54. "Utopia Rises Out of the Colombian Plains," *All Things Considered*.

55. White and Gonzalez Marino.

56. Ibid.

57. Ibid.

58. "Utopia Rises Out of the Colombian Plains," *All Things Considered*.

59. For more information, see Vandana Shiva, *Earth Democracy: Justice, Sustainability, and Peace*.

60. The International Forum on Globalization, *Alternatives to Economic Globalization*, 12.

61. Broadhead, 196.

Notes to conclusion

1. *The State of the World's Children 2005: Childhood Under Threat*, UNICEF.

2. *Human Development Report 1998*, United Nations Development Programme.

3. Marx, *Capital Vol 1*, 645.

4. George Monbiot, "You Say You Want A Revolution," *Globe and Mail*, 28 October 2006, F12.

5. McGregor, Sue L. T. "Consumerism as a Source of Structural Violence."

6. Ibid.

7. Monbiot.

8. Layard, "Happiness: Has Social Science a Clue?"

9. Ibid.

10. Robinson.

Notes to epilogue

1. Beginning in the mid-1990s, banks and mortgage companies approved increasing numbers of sub-prime mortgages to borrowers who could not qualify for conventional mortgages. In recent years, more and more of these borrowers began defaulting on the high-risk loans and the banks began foreclosing on homes, which burst the housing bubble as home values began to fall. Meanwhile, many people who had taken out home equity loans on the assumption that house prices would continue to rise suddenly found themselves owing more than their homes were worth after the crisis hit.

2. Yalman Onaran, "Wall Street Firms Cut 34,000 Jobs, Most Since 2001 Dot-Com Bust," Bloomberg, 24 March 2008. http://www.bloomberg.com/apps/news?pid=20601087&sid=aTARUhP3w5xE&refer=home.

3. Associated Press "U.S. government announces AIG bailout plan," CBC News, 16 September 2008. http://www.cbc.ca/money/story/2008/09/16/aig-bailout.html.

4. Louis Uchitelle, "U.S. Loses 533,000 Jobs in Biggest Drop Since 1974," *The New York Times*, 5 December 2008, http://www.nytimes.com/2008/12/06/business/economy/06jobs.html.

5. Don Lee, "Some owners deserting factories in China," *Los Angeles Times*, 3 November 2008, http://www.latimes.com/business/la-fi-factory3-2008nov03,0,7768849.story.

6. "Flaherty to Axe Subsidies to Political Parties in Fiscal Update: Sources," CBC News, 26 November 2008. http://www.cbc.ca/canada/story/2008/11/26/update-subsidy.html?ref=rss.

7. Brian Laghi, Daniel Leblanc and Campbell Clark, "Harper unfazed by market crisis," *Globe and Mail*, 15 September 2008. http://www.theglobeandmail.com/servlet/story/RTGAM.20080915.welxnmarkets0915/BNStory/politics/home.

8. Associated Press, "Canada's November job losses biggest in 26 years," MSN Money, 5 December 2008. http://news.moneycentral.msn.com/provider/providerarticle.aspx?feed=AP&date=20081205&id=9430519.

9. "World must act to fix worst crisis since 1929: Harper," CTV News, 22 November 2008. http://www.ctv.ca/servlet/ArticleNews/story/CT-VNews/20081122/apec_peru_081122/20081122.

10. "APEC Upbeat Over Global Downturn," BBC News, 23 November 2008. http://news.bbc.co.uk/2/hi/americas/7745059.stm.

11. "World must act to fix worst crisis since 1929: Harper," CTV News.

12. Stiglitz, "Capitalist Fools," *Vanity Fair*. http://www.vanityfair.com/magazine/2009/01/stiglitz200901.

13. Ibid.

14. Ibid.

15. Ibid.

16. Edmund L. Andrews, "Greenspan Concedes Error on Regulation," *The New York Times*, 23 October 2008. http://www.nytimes.com/2008/10/24/business/economy/24panel.html.

17. Manas Chakravarty, "Kafka and the Global Financial System," Live Mint, 30 December 2008. http://www.livemint.com/Articles/2008/12/30231658/Kafka-and-the-global-financial.html.

18. Sharon Otterman, "Republicans are resistant to Obama's stimulus plan," *The New York Times*, 25 January 2009, http://www.nytimes.com/2009/01/26/us/politics/26talkshow.html.

19. Hugh MacKenzie, "A backward-looking budget that looks supremely political," *Toronto Star*, 28 January 2009. http://www.thestar.com/comment/article/578264.

20. "Colombia reports sharp drop in remittances," Associated Press, 19 January 2009. http://www.boston.com/business/articles/2009/01/19/colombia_reports_sharp_drop_in_remittances/.

21. Stiglitz.

22. Doug Henwood, "Gloomy, w/ a 15% chance of depression," Left Business Observer, December 2008. http://www.leftbusinessobserver.com/Gloomy.html.

Bibliography

Action Canada. *Moving in the Right Direction? Labour Mobility, Labour Shortage and Canada's Human Potential.* June 2007.

Adams, Roy J. "Organizing Wal-Mart: The Canadian Campaign." *Just Labour,* Vol. 6 & 7 (2005): 1-11.

Amnesty International. *Colombia: The Paramilitaries in Medellín: Demobilization or Legalization?* September 2005.

Angus Reid Global Monitor. "Human Rights Trump Free Trade for Canadians." 20 July 2007. http://www.angus-reid.com/polls/view/human_rights_trump_free_trade_for_canadians/.

Arreaza, Teresa. "ALBA: Bolivarian Alternative for Latin America and the Caribbean," Venezuela Analysis, 30 January 2004. http://www.venezuelanalysis.com/analysis/339.

Bailey, Mark W. and Gordon Boyce. "The Manufacturing and Marketing of Steel in Canada: Dofasco Inc., 1912-1970," in *Business and Economic History,* edited by William J. Hausman, 229-36. Williamsburg, VA: College of William and Mary, 1989.

Banting, Keith G. "Do We Know Where We Are Going? The New Social Policy in Canada." *Canadian Public Policy,* 31, no.4 (2005): 421-29.

Barlow, Maude. *Too Close for Comfort: Canada's Future Within Fortress North America.* Toronto: McClelland and Stewart, 2005.

Barlow, Maude and Elizabeth May. *Frederick Street: Life and Death on Canada's Love Canal.* Toronto: HarperCollins, 2000.

Bennett, Hans. "Resisting Corporate Power in Colombia: An Interview with Aviva Chomsky," Dissident Voice, 5 February 2007. http://www.dissentvoice.org/Feb07/Bennett05.htm.

Bianco, Anthony. "No Union Please, We're Wal-Mart." *Business Week,* 13 February 2006. http://www.businessweek.com/magazine/content/06_07/b3971115.htm.

Bickerton, James and Teresa MacNeil. "Models of Development for Atlantic Canada," in *Doing Development Differently: Regional Development on the Atlantic Periphery,* edited by Susan Hodgett, David Johnson and Stephen A. Royle, 42-71. Sydney, NS: Cape Breton University Press, 2007.

BP. *BP Statistical Review of World Energy 2007.* June 2007.

Broadhead, Lee-Anne. *International Environmental Politics: The Limits of Green Diplomacy.* London: Lynne Rienner Publishers, 2002.

Bush, George W. "Press Conference of the President," The White House, 20 December 2006.

———. "Press Conference of the President," The White House, 28 February 2008.

Bush, George H. W. "Statement on Trade Initiatives for the Andean Region." George Bush Presidential Library and Museum. 1 November 1989. http://bushlibrary.tamu.edu/research/public_papers.php?id=1127&year=1989&month=11.

Canada. "Annual Labour Market Perspectives – Cape Breton 2006." Service Canada, 19 July 2006.

———. "Canada's New Government is Providing Real Tax Relief for Canadians," Finance Canada, 22 December 2006.

———. "Income Inequality and Redistribution in Canada: 1976 to 2004." Statistics Canada, May 2007.

———. "Industry Snapshot: Primary Steel in Canada," Industry Canada, 2000.

———. "Labour Market Review 2004 – Cape Breton." Service Canada, 6 July 2005.

———. "Federal Commercialization in Canada." Parliamentary Information and Research Group, 20 December 2005.

———. "Survey of Financial Security – 2005." Statistics Canada, 7 December 2006.

———. "University Tuition Fees." Statistics Canada, 18 October 2007.

———. "Canada and the North American Free Trade Agreement." Foreign Affairs and International Trade Canada. Accessed 2 February 2008.

Canadian Council of Chief Executives. "About CCCE," Canadian Council of Chief Executives. http://www.ceocouncil.ca/en/about/about.php. Accessed 14 October 2008.

Canadian Council on Social Development. "2001 Poverty Lines," 29 November 2002. http://www.ccsd.ca/factsheets/fs_lic01.htm.

Canmac Economics. *Socio-Economic Impact Analysis of the Tele-Service Industry on Cape Breton Island*, March 2003.

Chomsky, Aviva. *Linked Labor Histories: New England, Colombia and the Making of a Global Working Class.* Durham, NC: Duke University Press, 2008.

Clearwater Seafoods. *Strategies for the Long Term – 2005 Annual Report.* February 2006.

Clements, Barbara. "Starbucks Announces Its Earnings Set Record," *The News Tribune.* 16 November 2001, cited in Garry M. Leech, *Killing Peace: Colombia's Conflict and the Failure of U.S. Intervention.* New York: Information Network of the Americas, 2002.

Comisión Colombiano de Juristas, *Colombia 2002-2006: Situación de derechos humanos y derecho humanitario,* January 2007.

———. *Colombia: En contravía de las recomendaciones internacionales sobre derechos humanos, Balance de la política de seguridad democrática y la situación de derechos humanos y derecho humanitario, agosto 2002 a agosto 2004,* 15 October 2004.

DeRoche, Constance. "Culture of Poverty Lives On: Community Economic Developers in Cape Breton, Nova Scotia." *City & Society* 25, no. 2 (2003): 225-54.

Dodds, Colin, and Ronald Colman, "Income Distribution in Nova Scotia, 2000," in *From the net to the Net: Atlantic Canada and the Global Economy,* edited by James Sacouman and Henry Veltmeyer, 63-83. Aurora, ON: Garamond Press, 2005.

Drummond Company, Inc., "About Us: Community," Drummond Company, Inc. http://www.drummondco.com/about/Community.aspx. Accessed 14 October 2008.

Dyer, Simon, Jeremy Morehouse, Katie Laufenburg and Rob Powell. "Under-Mining the Environment: The Oil Sands Report Card." The Pembina Institute, January 2008. http://pubs.pembina.org/reports/OS-Undermining-Final.pdf.

Emera. *2004 Annual Financial Report*, 11 February 2005.

Enterprise Cape Breton Corporation. "ECBC Program Guidelines." http://www.ecbc.ca/e/PDFs/ECBC%20Guidelines%20Ecommerce%2008.pdf. Accessed 16 January 2008)

———. "Project Information Site." http://atip.ecbc-secb.gc.ca/projects/e/content/default.asp. Accessed 17 October 2008.

———. "Stream to Establish 900-Job Centre at Glace Bay," 10 August 2001. http://www.ecbc-secb.gc.ca/e/newsreleases/20010810.asp.

"Entrevista con José Armando Zamora, director de la ANH." *Carta Petrolera*, August-October 2003. http://www.ecopetrol.com.co/especiales/carta/entrevista.htm.

Ferguson, Brian. *The Potential of Private Sector Health Care in Canada*. Canadian Health Care Consensus Group, October 2007.

Flannery, Tim. *The Weather Makers: How We Are Changing the Climate and What It Means for Life on Earth*. Toronto: HarperCollins, 2005.

Flóres, Carmen Elisa. "Migration and the Urban Informal Sector in Colombia." conference paper, June 2003. http://pum.princeton.edu/pumconference/papers/4-Florez.pdf.

Frank, David. *J.B. McLachlan: A Biography: The Story of a Legendary Labour Leader and the Cape Breton Coal Miners*. Toronto: James Lorimer, 1999.

Gaceta Oficial de la República Bolivariana de Venezuela. "Decreta con Fuerza de Ley Organica de Hidrocarburos," 13 November 2001.

Gibbs, Terry. "Business as Unusual: What the Chávez Era Tells Us About Democracy Under Globalisation." *Third World Quarterly* 27, no.2 (2006): 265-79.

Good, Tom and Joan McFarland. "Call Centres: A New Solution to an Old Problem," in *From the net to the Net: Atlantic Canada and the Global Economy*, edited by James Sacouman and Henry Veltmeyer, 99-113. Aurora, Ontario: Garamond Press, 2005.

Gulli, Cathy and Kate Lunau. "Adding Fuel to the Doctor Crisis," *Maclean's*, 2 January 2008. http://www.macleans.ca/science/health/article.jsp?content=20080102_122329_6200.

Heisz, Andrew. "Income Inequality and Redistribution in Canada: 1976 to 2004." Statistics Canada, May 2007.

Heron, Craig. *Working in Steel: The Early Years in Canada, 1883-1935*. Toronto: McClelland and Stewart, 1988.

Higgs, Robert. "The Trillion-Dollar Defense Budget Is Already Here." The Independent Institute, 15 March 2007. http://www.independent.org/newsroom/article.asp?id=1941.

Hull, Dennis N. "The Role of Geology in the Management of Ohio's Solid Waste," Ohio Department of Natural Resources, 20 April 2005. http://www.dnr.state.oh.us/geosurvey/gen/environment/Manage/tabid/7913/Default.aspx.

IMPACT Fund. "IMPACT Fund: Investment Management of Portfolios in Atlantic Canada Training." St. Mary's University. http://www.stmarys.ca/academic/sobey/Impact/welcome.html. Accessed 17 February 2008.

———. "Letter from the Dean." St. Mary's University. http://www.stmarys.ca/academic/sobey/Impact/dean.html. Accessed 17 February 2008.

Innis, Harold. *The Cod Fisheries: The History of an International Economy*. Toronto: Ryerson, 1940.

International Confederation of Trade Unions (ICFTU), *Annual Survey of Violations of Trade Union Rights – 2006*, 7 June 2006.

The International Forum on Globalization. *Alternatives to Economic Globalization: A Better World Is Possible*. San Francisco: Berrett-Koehler, 2002.

International Labour Organisation, *C169 Indigenous and Tribal Peoples Convention, 1989*, 26 June 1989.

Isacson, Adam. "The 2000-2001 Colombia Aid Package By the Numbers." Center for International Policy. 5 July 2000. http://www.ciponline.org/colombia/aidcompare.htm.

Juarez, Carlos E. "Trade and Development Policies in Colombia: Export Promotion and Outward Orientation, 1967-1992." *Studies in Comparative and International Development*, 28, no.3 (1993): 67-97.

Kealey, Gregory S. *Workers and Canadian History*. Montreal: McGill-Queen's University Press, 1995.

Kennedy, Martin. *Fish Plant Workers Responding to Globalization in North Sydney, Cape Breton*. Partnerships in Learning. January 2008.

Kohler, Nicholas. "Danny Williams Picks His Battles," *Maclean's*, 31 July 2006. http://www.macleans.ca/canada/national/article.jsp?content=20060731_130820_130820.

KPMG. *Competitive Alternatives: KPMG's Guide to International Business Costs*, 2006.

Lateline. "FTA is Not Free or Fair, Says Hargrove." Australian Broadcasting Corporation. 27 July 2004. http://www.abc.net.au/lateline/content/2004/s1163313.htm.

Layard, Richard. "Happiness: Has Social Science a Clue?" Lionel Robbins Memorial Lectures. March 2003. http://cep.lse.ac.uk/events/lectures/layard/RL030303.pdf.

Leatherdale, Linda. "The Bell Tolls," Canoe Money, 2 February 2006. http://money.canoe.ca/Columnists/Leatherdale/2006/02/02/1423151-sun.html.

Leech, Garry. *Crude Interventions: The United States, Oil and the New World (Dis)Order.* London: Zed Books, 2006.

———. *Killing Peace: Colombia's Conflict and the Failure of U.S. Intervention.* New York: Inota, 2002.

LeFort, Jean-Yves. "Energy Revenues: Are Canadians Getting Fleeced?" Council of Canadians, 23 October 2007. http://www.canadians.org/energy/documents/Royalty_Report_07.pdf.

Lipton, Charles. *The Trade Union Movement of Canada 1827-1959.* Montreal: Canadian Social Publications, 1967.

Lustgarten, Abrahm. "The Dark Magic of Oil Sands." *Fortune,* 3 October 2005. http://money.cnn.com/magazines/fortune/fortune_archive/2005/10/03/8356746/index.htm.

MacAuley, Scott. "Contradictions in Community Economic Development: New Dawn Enterprises," in *From the net to the Net: Atlantic Canada and the Global Economy,* edited by James Sacouman and Henry Veltmeyer, 115-36. Aurora, ON: Garamond, 2005.

MacEachern, George. *George MacEachern: An Autobiography: The Story of a Cape Breton Labour Radical.* Sydney, NS: University College of Cape Breton Press, 1987.

MacEwan, Paul. *Miners and Steelworkers: Labour in Cape Breton.* Toronto: Hakkert and Company, 1976.

MacNeil, Suzanne. "Reflections on Mining in Colombia: When 'Development' Creates Deprivation," *Colombia Journal,* 13 August 2007. http://www.colombiajournal.org/colombia262.htm.

Macklem, Katherine. "A Steel City's Blues." *Maclean's.* 21 June 2004, 30-32.

———. "Shifting Into Reverse," *Maclean's.* 23 September 2002, 30-32.

Martinez, Ibsen. "Panama: Does Geography Matter?" The Library of Economics and Liberty, 4 February 2008. http://www.econlib.org/library/Columns/y2008/MartinezPanama.html.

Marx, Karl. *Capital Vol 1.* Moscow: Foreign Languages, 1961.

Maybarduk, Peter. "A Peoples Health System: Venezuela Works to Bring Health Care to the Excluded." Multinational Monitor. October 2004. http://multinationalmonitor.org/mm2004/102004/maybarduk.html.

McGregor, Sue L. T. "Consumerism as a Source of Structural Violence." The Human Sciences Working Papers Archive. 2003. http://www.kon.org/HSwp/archive/consumerism.pdf.

Mesa Toro, Emiro and Manuel Reina Salgado. *Notes on Economic and Labor Factors in Colombia 2005.* National Union School (ENS), October 2005.

"Minister: IMF, Multilateral Banks Have Impoverished Latin America," *Hoover's Online,* 5 March 2002, cited in Garry M. Leech, *Killing Peace: Colombia's Conflict and the Failure of U.S. Intervention.* New York: Information Network of the Americas, 2002.

Moberg, David. "Stuck in the Middle," In These Times, 5 May 2003. http://www .inthesetimes.com/article/582/.

Mommer, Bernard. "Subversive Oil," in *Venezuelan Politics in the Chávez Era: Class, Polarization and Conflict,* edited by Steve Ellner and Daniel Hellinger, 131-45. Boulder: Lynne Rienner, 2003.

Murphy, Jamie. "Hanging Out the Welcome Sign," *Time,* 24 December 1984. http://www.time.com/time/magazine/article/0,9171,951396-3,00.html.

Newell, Peter. "Citizenship, Accountability and Community: The Limits of the CSR Agenda." *International Affairs,* 81, no.3 (2005): 541-57.

Nova Scotia. Department of Finance. "2006 Census of Canada: Nova Scotia Perspective," March 2006.

Nova Scotia. Department of Finance. "Nova Scotia Labour Market – December 2005." 6 January 2006.

Nova Scotia. Department of Health. "Moving to Address High Cancer Rates in Cape Breton," 21 April 1999.

Olgilve, Kelvin K. *From Public U to Private U: An Atlantic Canadian Opportunity.* Atlantic Institute for Market Studies, September 2005.

Owens, Jeffrey. *Fundamental Tax Reform: The Experience of OECD Countries.* The OECD's Centre for Tax Policy and Administration, February 2005.

The Pembina Institute. "Misdirected Spending: Groups Demand Investigation into Billions in Federal Subsidies to Canada's Booming Oil and Gas Industry." 3 October 2005. http://www.pembina.org/media-release/1154.

Plataforma Colombiana de Derechos Humanos, Democracia y Desarrollo. *El Embrujo Autoritario: Primer Año de Gobierno de Álvaro Uribe Vélez,* September 2003.

Ramírez Cuellar, Francisco. *The Profits of Extermination: How U.S. Corporate Power is Destroying Colombia.* Monroe, ME: Common Courage, 2005.

Robinson, William I. "What is Critical Globalization Studies? Intellectual Labor and Global Society," in *Public Sociologies Reader,* edited by Judith R. Blau and Keri Iyall-Smith, 21-36. Lanham, MA: Rowman and Littlefield, 2006.

Sacouman, James. "Capitalist Restructuring on Canada's East Coast," in *From the net to the Net: Atlantic Canada and the Global Economy,* edited by James Sacouman and Henry Veltmeyer, 51-62. Aurora, ON: Garamond, 2005.

Saez, Emmanuel and Michael R. Veall. "The Evolution of High Incomes in Northern America: Lessons from Canadian Evidence." *The American Economic Review,* 95, no.3 (2005): 831-49.

Shiva, Vandana. *Earth Democracy: Justice, Sustainability, and Peace.* Cambridge, MA: South End Press, 2005.

Shiva, Vandana. "New Emperors, Old Clothes," *The Ecologist,* 1 July 2005. http:// www.theecologist.org/pages/archive_detail.asp?content_id=447.

Sinclair, Scott. *Atlantica: Myths and Reality.* Canadian Centre for Policy Alternatives, February 2007.

Steedman, Mercedes. "The Changing Face of the Call Centre Industry in Canada." United Steelworkers – Canadian National Office, September 2003. http://www.usw.ca/program/content/1621.php.

Straszheim, Donald H. "The Economic Impact of Growth in China," *CFA Institute Conference Proceedings Quarterly* 23, no.1 (2006): 88-93.

United Nations. *Human Development Report 2006*. United Nations Development Programme, 2006.

———. *Human Development Report 1998*. United Nations Development Programme, 1998.

———. *The State of the World's Children 2005: Childhood Under Threat*. UNICEF, December 2004.

United States. "Monthly U.S. Crude Oil and Petroleum Products Imports from Canada." Department of Energy, 24 January 2008. http://tonto.eia.doe.gov/dnav/pet/hist/mttimusca1m.htm. Accessed 20 December 2007.

U.S. Office on Colombia, *Paramilitary Demobilization*. Accessed 15 December 2007.

———. "Venezuela: Country Report on Human Rights Practices for 1998." Department of State. 26 February 1999.

Uribe, Alvaro. "Palabras del Presidente Uribe en posesión de nuevo comandante de la FAC." *Colombia: Presidencia de la República*. 8 September 2003. http://www.presidencia.gov.co/prensa_new/discursos/fac.htm.

The Vanier Institute of the Family. *The Current State of Canadian Family Finances – 2007 Report*, 11 February 2008.

Wal-Mart Stores, Inc. *2006 Annual Report: Building Smiles*. February 2006.

Wal-Mart Stores, Inc. "Canada Fact Sheet," August 2008. http://walmartstores.com/download/1998.pdf.

Weisbrot, Mark. "Poverty Reduction in Venezuela: A Reality-Based View." *ReVista: Harvard Review of Latin America* 8, no.1 (2008): 1-8.

Weisman, Alan. "Colombia's Model City." *In Context: A Quarterly of Humane Sustainable Culture*. Fall 1995. http://www.context.org/ICLIB/IC42/Colombia.htm.

White, Richard E. and Gloria Eugenia Gonzalez Marino. "Las Gaviotas: Sustainability in the Tropics." *World Watch Magazine*. Online at Access My Library. 1 May 2007. http://www.accessmylibrary.com/coms2/summary_0286-31746133_ITM.

Workman, Thom. *Social Torment: Globalization in Atlantic Canada*. Black Point, NS: Fernwood, 2003.

The World Bank Group. *Colombia Poverty Report*, March 2002.

Yao, Yuanming Alvin. "China's Oil Strategy and Its Implications for U.S.-China Relations." *Issues & Studies* 42, no.3 (2006): 165-201.

Index

Cape Breton (NS): coal and steel industries, 13, 20-30, 41-45; community economic development, 106-07, 108; deindustrialization, 41-45; fish-processing plants, 21, 86-87; health crisis, 44-45; militant labour struggles, 23-30; out-migrations, 74-75; service industry, 17, 74-83
Cape Breton Power, 103
Cape Breton Regional Municipality, 74-75
Cape Breton University, 98
capitalism: profit and growth imperatives, 15, 16, 106, 119-20, 133, 146. See also, global capitalist model
capitalist elites, 14; in Colombia, 49-50, 52, 57, 72, 108, 134; and Fordist compact, 35, 146; and global North, 36, 56, 70, 71, 87, 100; and government bailouts, 140, 146-47; political and regulatory controls, 23, 26, 45-46, 108-09, 118, 123-24, 134; and a responsibility program, 119-20; rhetorics of, 15, 36-37, 74, 78, 84, 102, 132-33, 139, 144; in Venezuela, 110-11, 113, 118. See also global capitalist model; neoliberalism
Carbones de Colombia, (Carbocol), 65
Carroll, Billy, 26
CBRM. See Cape Breton Regional Municipality
CCCE. See Canadian Council of Chief Executives
CCF. See Co-operative Commonwealth Federation
CED. See Cape Breton (NS): community economic development
CERI. See Canadian Energy Research Institute
Cerrejón Foundation, 67
Cerrejón Mine Company, 16, 47, 65-72
Chakravarty, Manas, 143-44
Chancleta (CO), 67
Chávez, Hugo, 89, 92; reforms of, 110-14, 118
ChevronTexaco, 91
"Chicago Boys," 37
child poverty: in Atlantic Canada, 94
Chile, 37, 113
China. See neoliberalism in China

Chiquita Brands, 61
Chomsky, Aviva, 65-66, 69
Chrétien, Jean, 39, 80, 94
Chronicle Herald, 77
CIDA. See Canadian International Development Agency
Citco Group, 80
Clearwater Seafoods, 86-87
Coady, Moses (Father), 32
coal industry. See Cape Breton (NS): coal and steel industries
coal miners. See Cape Breton (NS): militant labour struggles
Coca-Cola Company, 61
coca cultivation, 50, 51, 53, 58, 73
coffee trade, 50-52, 72
Colombia. See coffee trade; Columbian army; community displacements; import substitution industrialization; National Front; neoliberalism in Colombia; Plan Colombia
Colombia-Canada relations, 63-64, 58-69, 108-09, 142
Colombia Goldfields and Coalcorp, 63
Colombian army, 52-53, 58, 62, 72; services to Cerrejón Mine Company, 66-67, 69; services to Drummond Company, 60-61
Colombian Commission of Jurists, 62, 150n6
Colombian Communist Party, 49, 150n1
Columbian Ministry of Mines, 63
Colombian State Mineworkers' Union. See Sintraminercol
Committee to Relocate Tabaco, 66-67
community displacements, 52, 59, 64; and Chancleta, 67; and Tabaco, 47, 65-71, 72
Conquistador Mines, 63
consumer capitalism. See global capitalist model: consumerism and happiness
Convergys Corp., 80, 83
Co-operative Commonwealth Federation, 34-35
corporate welfare programs. See bailouts and stimulus packages
corporations. See privatization: of state-owned corporations
Council of Canadians, 40, 90
credit crunch, 140

Crowley, Brian Lee, 95
Cruz, Francisco Javier, 59
"culture of dependency," 106

Day, Brian, 96
death squads, 60, 61
debt. See neoliberalism: and debt creation
deindustrialization, 14, 41-45, 76, 78, 82
Dell Computer Corp., 82-83
demobilization. See paramilitaries:
  demobilization of
Department of Economic Development
  and Tourism (NB), 79
Department of La Guaajira (CO): and
  Cerrejón Mine 65, 68; Columbian
  army, 69; description of, 71; dirty war,
  72
Department of Vichada (CO), 124
deRoche, Constance, 32, 40-41, 105-07
DEVCO. See Cape Breton Development
  Corporation
dirty war, 47, 52-53, 60, 72
DISCO. See Dominion Iron and Steel
  Company
District 26. See United Mine Workers of
  America
Dodds, Alex, 98
Dominion Coal Company, 21, 24
Dominion Iron and Steel Company,
  21-23
Dominion Steel and Coal Corporation,
  41
DOSCO. See Dominion Steel and Coal
  Corporation
Dougherty, David, 83
Dow Jones Industrial Average, 139, 140
Drummond Company, 59-63
DynCorp, 57

"earth democracy," 129-30
ECBC. See Enterprise Cape Breton
  Corporation
economic refugees. See community
  displacements
Ecopetrol, 56
Ecuador, 117, 134-35
Edmonton (AB), 82-83
education. See under neoliberalism in
  Canada; Sweden; Venezuela
Employment Insurance, 38-39, 93

energy policies. See under neoliberalism
  in Canada; neoliberalism in Colombia;
  Venezuela
Enterprise Cape Breton Corporation,
  103-04
environment: and Drummond Company,
  62-63; and economic growth, 119-121
  133; and greenhouse gas emissions, 45,
  91, 120; and regulations, 64; and toxic
  waste, 44-45
Evans, Jackie, 86-87
Export Development Bank of Canada,
  65
ExxonMobil, 65, 90, 91, 98
Eyking, Mark, 87

Fabricio Ojeda complex, 116
FARC, 52-53, 150n6
Ferguson, Brian, 95-96
fish-processing plants, 20, 86-87
Fordist compact: described as, 30-31. See
  also, Keynesian policy framework
Fort McMurray (AB), 91
Friedman, Milton, 36, 37
Fuerzas Armades Revolucionarias de
  Colombia. See FARC

García, Rafael, 60
Garzón, Angelino, 56
Gaviria, César, 50
Germany, 141
Glass-Steagall Act, 142
Glencore International, 65
global capitalist model: consumer and
  consumption, 120-21, 131-32, 133,
  135-36, 143; and happiness, 128, 138-
  39; ecological limits to, 15-16, 45, 88-
  92, 119-21, 133; flaws of the system,
  71, 119, 133, 142, 143, 146; and fossil
  fuel dependencies, 17, 45, 119, 123,
  124, 130, 143; and military-industrial
  complex, 57; and poverty, 70-71, 145;
  and social inequality, 131-33; and
  surplus labour, 17, 22-23, 29, 39, 55,
  76, 87, 140. See also, capitalist elites;
  neoliberalism
global North: and capitalist elites, 36,
  56, 70, 71, 108; and the global South,
  13-14, 18, 46, 48-49, 56, 70, 74, 76, 92,
  111, 129; and standard of living, 72,

Ramírez, Francisco: assassination attempts on, 64, 68
Rand, Ayn, 142
Reagan, Ronald, 19, 37, 142
Regina Manifesto, 35
"relative deprivation," 136-37
remittance-based economy, 14, 55-56, 75, 145
Revolutionary Armed Forces of Colombia. See FARC
Richardson, Bill, 53-54, 58
Robinson, William I., 15-16, 98, 139-40
Roes, Eric, 86
Roosevelt, Franklin Delano, 144
Royal Commission on the Coal Mining Industry in Nova Scotia, 29-30
royalties. See oil royalty rates
Ruiz, Louisa, 117

Saez, Emmanuel, 93-94
Sault Ste. Marie (ON): and Algoma Steel Plant, 43; shift to service industry, 82
secretary of energy (U.S.). See Richardson, Bill
Scotia Capital, 141
Security and Prosperity Partnership of North America, 39
Service Canada: Labour Market Review 2004 – Cape Breton, 75
service industry, 75-86
Servicom, 80
Shiva, Vandana: and "earth democracy," 129-30, 158n59; on economic growth, 119-20; on poverty, 70
Sintramienergetica, 60, 62
Sintraminercol, 64
Sobey School of Business, 99
society-to-society barter, 114
Soler Mora, Gustavo: assassination of, 60
Sotillo, Arnaldo, 116
St. Mary's University, 99
stagflation, 36-37
staples theory, 20
Starbucks, 52
Statistics Canada: and Employment Insurance, 38; and income equality, 93; and personal savings, 102
steel industry. See Cape Breton (NS): coal and steel industries

steelworkers. See Cape Breton (NS): militant labour struggles
Stiglitz, Joseph, 142, 147
sub-prime mortgage crisis, 139, 143
subsidies. See call centres; neoliberalism: and subsidies
Suncor Energy Inc., 90
Sweden: and education, 100-01
Sydney (NS): and police district, 27; and population of, 21, 44
Sydney Post, 26, 28
Sydney Record, 24-25
Sydney Steel Corporation, 41
Sydney Tar Ponds, 44-45
sympathy strike, 27-29
Syncrude Canada Ltd., 90
SYSCO. See Sydney Steel Corporation

Tabaco (CO), 16; community displacement of, 47, 65-67, 68-71
taxes: and corporations, 39, 76-77, 79, 83, 154n50; and oil industry, 89, 90, 110; and personal income, 93. See also, goods and services tax
TeleTech, 80
Textron Inc., 57
Thatcher, Margaret, 19, 37, 96, 102
Tissot, Roger, 110
TLC. Trades and Labour Congress of Canada, 30, 31, 35
Trudeau, Pierre, 88

UFCW. See United Food and Commercial Workers Union
UMWA. See United Mine Workers of America
UNDP. See United Nations Development Programme
UNICEF, 131
United Farmers of Nova Scotia Party, 25
United Food and Commercial Workers Union, 84, 85-86
United Mine Workers of America, 24, 25, 28, 30, 68
United Nations Development Programme, 124, 131
United Self-Defence Forces of Colombia: demobilization of, 61-62
United States: banking and investment sectors, 139, 142; and Canadian oil,

About the authors

Terry Gibbs is an assistant professor of Political Science and director of the Centre for International Studies at Cape Breton University. She specializes in issues related to democracy and globalization. Gibbs is a contributor to the book *New Perspectives on Globalization and Antiglobalization: Prospects for a New World Order* (Ashgate Publishing, 2008) and her articles have been published in various journals.

Garry Leech is an independent journalist and editor of *Colombia Journal* (www.colombiajournal.org). He is the author of several books, including *Beyond Bogotá: Diary of a Drug War Journalist in Colombia* (Beacon Press, 2009) and *Crude Interventions: The United States, Oil and the New World (Dis)Order* (Zed Books, 2006). He is also the co-author of *The People Behind Colombian Coal: Mining, Multinationals and Human Rights* (Pisando Callos, 2007). Leech is a lecturer in Political Science at Cape Breton University.

Praise for Terry Gibbs and Garry Leech's
The Failure of Global Capitalism:
From Cape Breton to Colombia and Beyond

Maude Barlow
National Chairperson of The Council of Canadians
Author of *Blue Gold: The Fight to Stop Corporate Theft of the World's Water*
(W. W. Norton, 2005)

"What do Cape Breton and Colombia have in common? Decades of life under a market economy that gobbles resources for the benefit of the few based on back breaking work of the many. Now, they also have Garry Leech and Terry Gibbs who have written a scathing book chronicling this unjust system and pointing the way to a better Cape Breton, a better Colombia and a better world."

William I. Robinson,
Professor of Sociology, Global Studies and Latin American Studies
University of California at Santa Barbara
Author of *Latin America and Global Capitalism: A Critical Globalization Perspective*, (Johns Hopkins University Press, 2008).

"This book is a well-researched and shocking exposure of the ugly tapestry of oppression, inequality and environmental degradation that global capitalism has woven from Canada to Colombia and beyond. Gibbs and Leech are deft at showing the connections between the local and the global and the consequent need to act both locally and globally if we are to confront the depredations of the system.

But they don't stop at demonstrating the failure of global capitalism; they show how local communities are struggling for alternatives that point the way toward a more democratic, equitable and sustainable future. This book is a fine piece of scholarship and a must read for community activists, social movements and committed scholars."

CPSIA information can be obtained at www.ICGtesting.com
Printed in the USA
LVOW100654030812

292784LV00001B/168/P